Phantoms of the Soap Operas

Also by Jenny Randles

(From Robert Hale)

UFOs: A British Viewpoint (with Peter Warrington)
UFO Study: A Handbook for Enthusiasts
UFO Reality: A Critical Look at the Physical Evidence
Beyond Explanation?: Paranormal Experiences of Famous
    People
Sixth Sense: Psychic Powers and Your Five Senses
Abduction

Phantoms
of the
Soap Operas

... and Other Showbiz Enigmas

Jenny Randles

ROBERT HALE · LONDON

Robert Hale Limited
Clerkenwell House
Clerkenwell Green
London EC1R 0HT

British Library Cataloguing in Publication Data

Randles, Jenny, *1951*–
Phantoms of the soap operas
1. Television studies. Ghosts
I. Title
133.1'22

ISBN 0-7090-3713-9

Photoset in Palatino by
Derek Doyle & Associates, Mold, Clwyd.
Printed in Great Britain by
St Edmundsbury Press Ltd, Bury St Edmunds, Suffolk.
Bound by WBC Bookbinders Limited.

Contents

Author's Note

This is a book about strange things that have happened in the lives of television personalities. You will meet many kinds of phantoms, from those which haunt our dreams and foretell the future, to spooks and spectres that may suggest a life after death. The paranormal also contains some bizarre apparitions, including ghostly visions and alien glows that dart across the sky.

Many weird tales have been told about the supernatural, but usually the story-tellers are strangers, merely names that fill the pages of a book. Not so in these pages. Each anecdote comes from someone who has made frequent appearances on TV screens around the world. Mostly these are actors or actresses, often from the shows that have become labelled 'soap operas' since the early days when such serializations had their meagre budgets sponsored by American soap-manufacturers.

Things are different now. Precisely what is, or is not, a 'soap' is open to personal interpretation.

This book surveys all sorts of popular TV programmes, from a liberal sprinkling of the traditional soap to the drama and adventure serials and some lighter offerings. There is plenty here to please all types of viewer.

We hope that you will be suitably amazed.

Phantoms of the Soap Operas

Opening Titles

The world is full of strange stories. Wherever you look, you will find them: in shops and supermarkets, pubs and meeting-places. The paranormal is a modern buzz-word that attracts listeners to a conversation like midges to a summer lawn. Just one whiff of a UFO, ghost or something going bump in the night and we all get hooked.

Why do these phenomena fascinate us so much? Perhaps they are the last echoes of the myth and fairy tale that linger within our minds, a half-forgotten dream from childhood that we dare not sacrifice to the spectre of old age. In this increasingly computerized society, it may be heresy to judge from ESP instead of digital read-outs, or look for flying saucers in the sky amidst the jumbo jets, and yet the world is awash with heretics, for most of us toy with these concepts at one time or another.

At least some good comes from this. It destroys the illusion that powerful scientists and number-crunching bureaucrats have the world sewn up in their mathematical equations. There *are* things which even a PhD with all the megabytes in the universe behind him still cannot resolve. But someone else, alone in bed, with just imagination and intuition for company, *might* succeed. Doesn't that leave a warm glow in the spirit?

In short, all this psychic nonsense restores a place in the scheme of things for the ordinary man and woman. We can all be gifted. Anyone can see a phantom or have a dream that foretells the future. You do not need certificates coming out of your ears and an IQ that would do credit to MENSA. Indeed, as experience shows, such attributes are sometimes a disadvantage, for those forever asking questions often end up concluding that there are no answers. And to most scientists, something without an answer is a nightmare.

Yet there is a deeper meaning to these things as well. Remember those bedtime stories where the young girl or boy was led on tiptoes into the enchanted forest? It may be that, like many such tales, these are really deep allegories. The enchanted forest is the wonderland that all things supernatural represent. And if we presume to cast aside convention and step into the magic glades, we feel the excitement prickle through our senses. We taste that wonderful expectancy that comes only when most things are new and nothing is deemed impossible. For in the psychic universe, nothing is.

Well, almost nothing.

At least the stranger shores of our hidden world make us face up to the issues that too easily disappear when we have to worry about paying bills and making suppers. It is hard juggling the nature of the universe or the existence of God along with the time of the next bus and the need to get to the office before the boss does. Yet, every now and then, we must stand aside and do just that, for there are fundamental problems waiting to be confronted. Run away from them and you go through life only half-awake.

For instance: if we can dream about the future, is it mapped out for us or can we change our destiny?

If UFOs are real, does that mean that there are other lifeforms out there who have not made such a hash of things and can offer 'godly' advice?

And if people see ghosts, is that because part of us never dies but lives on in some other dimension with mysterious, even divine, purpose?

The paranormal prises open creaky doors laced with cobwebs, behind which we can find these problems and maybe some of their solutions. Doubtless we each have our suspicions of what we would like these answers to be, and the image may flit through our minds that wishful thinking is hardly the same as a proven fact. But so what? It is the teasing provocation – the possibility – that excites. These may be the greatest delusions we will ever know, but if they are, who is the poorer because of them?

Think about it. We slide through seventy-odd years,

growing older by the second. When we begin to understand what all the fuss is about, we also comprehend our own mortality. That is the most daunting, terrifying thing any of us has to square up to. And we all must face it, sooner or later.

The paranormal offers a glint of hope, a faint murmur that a humdrum life may not be all there is. Perhaps we are in a long-term learning-process and it's just the first day of school.

You have two ways of responding to that concept. You can do what most of us do and be cheered by the rebellious image that materialism and our own mortality *could* prove to be the illusion, or you can fight the tide, as those who call themselves realists seem to require. To them the paranormal is a threat. It creates a belief in things that cannot be true and sets up false anticipations. So they see it as their duty to protect us from the fantasy-mongers and myth-makers who churn out such tales.

Both those names have been waved in front of me on more than one occasion. I rarely mind. I have a swift and devastating answer to the charge. It is this. If I am wrong, then all I have done is offered people a few seeds of an idea and made their journey down the rocky road a bit more interesting. When we reach the end, something or nothing is waiting for each one of us. If it is something, then those who ponder the meaning of the paranormal will at least be prepared. If it is nothing, it is scarcely going to matter much, is it?

What do these sceptics, or debunkers, or rationalists provide us with? Reality, they claim. But ask any true scientist to define 'reality' and you will hear answers that sound suspiciously like a cross between God and ESP.

The realists can only burst balloons and spoil the party, spreading doom, gloom and despondency for no valid reason that I can see. If they are wrong in their sombre pronunciations that we are little more than an ape with a few GCEs, then the greatest shock of their afterlife is waiting down the line. If they are right (and there can only be a 50/50 chance of that), they won't even have the satisfaction of saying 'I told you so.'

If anything is a reason for giving the paranormal a fair

chance, that seems to be it, all wrapped up for you.

So that is what this little book is all about. It is a set of fairy stories for grown-ups. I do not know how many of them are true, or even if any of them are true, but I think it very likely that most of the people who relate them are sincere, although they may well be no more wise than you or I as to what 'being true' actually means in this instance.

What this book is *not* can be stated just as readily. You will find little objective analysis of these claims, no pontification or attempts to prove my own theories. At times I will direct you toward a deeper text. Indeed, I have written some analytical studies myself. But this is a book of curiosities to dip into from time to time. You do not have to believe or disbelieve a single word. You have my permission just to wonder.

Of course, books of spooky stories are not exactly new, so I have (to use a much-loved phrase) come up with a gimmick. I do not mind that word being applied here, although do not be misled by it.

The collection of tales is built around one group of people – the stars of popular television shows. It is reasonable to ask why.

One answer would be: because that was an interesting thing to do. But more importantly it helps you identify with what is going on. Simply because the paranormal has become commonplace, it can occasionally be a little underwhelming to hear another anecdote about a total stranger who claims something extraordinary. That special flavour of awe and mystification is what puts the 'super' into the supernatural. By telling famous people's stories, you do avoid turning it into something trite and 'natural'.

TV personalities adopt such a large posture in most people's lives that they become the next best thing to one of the family. A name in a book would mean nothing to you, but if your mother or father, brother or sister were to say that this thing had happened to them, that would make you sit up straight and pay attention. So a claim by a TV performer adds spice and zest, plus a touch of credibility. After that, the story might take root.

However, there is an even more fundamental reason

why I have adopted this approach. It is best illustrated by quoting one or two actors (I shall use this term throughout to mean male and female actors).

That wonderful serious thespian Sidney Poitier once described how he gets into a part: he reads the script, tries to absorb all the person's habits and needs, then, 'I now have the man in total. I know what his reaction would be to everything done … I walk on the stage and it happens … you perform, because what begins to happen out there is that you find that you have taken on the milieu of the character …'[1]

In other words, Poitier tells us, an actor absorbs every aspect of the part he is playing (be it a real character or a fictional one). So complete is this process that he *becomes* who he plays during that time on the stage or the set. In order to do this, he has had to breathe in the life force and drink of the emotions that create this other entity.

That tells us something very important. As does an experience of Dorothy Tutin, the famous character actress.

She was starring in a play called *The Devils*, where she had to act out a horrific scene involving pure submission to evil. The role was tested in front of a group of nuns, so that Dorothy could experiment, and this is what happened: 'I just made my mind a blank and tried to imagine possession. The extraordinary thing was that the nuns picked it up and in fact we had the experience that happened in the actual play, in that nunnery, a sort of catching hysteria.'[2]

The very act of playing the part became sufficiently realistic that things started to happen in the way playwright John Whiting had imagined them. The nuns 'tuned in' to the emotions of Dorothy Tutin and her suffering, sharing in them both.

American Emmy-winning actress Jane Alexander, whose masterful TV skills range over the entire spectrum of human life, from Eleanor Roosevelt to a Nazi death-camp survivor, explains that she has trained so hard to absorb herself within another being that the emotions of that person begin to take her over completely. When acting a role, she too can almost become 'possessed' by the spirit of the character, both on and off screen.

Together these experiences point up the crucial importance of emotion and absorption to the acting profession. It is necessary to *feel* the part in order to play it, and this can have peculiar side-effects. The emotions can leak out and infest an audience when the acting is first-rate. Some observers may cry during a truly good portrayal, for example.

But why is any of that relevant to the paranormal? Because in writing a previous book about ESP I discovered that everywhere I looked there was one clue that kept staring me in the face. The key to these various strange phenomena was the emotional link between the subject of the event (be it a dream premonition or a ghost) and the person who shares in it. When the link is strong, the experience flows. When it is not, ESP is far less likely.[3]

I trust you now see my point. Actors use emotion and enter into a kind of 'sponge mode', soaking in a warm bathtub of feeling and empathy. This same facility lies at the heart of the paranormal, so we might predict that actors would have more than their fair share of psychic experience.

And they do. Here is just one example of what I mean.

The reporter is a man from a Yorkshire city. I shall just call him Neville, as he prefers that I do not name him, because he does not wish the story to seem like a publicity stunt. Neville has appeared in a number of TV soaps and series as an actor but is professionally best known as a singer with a group that has recorded hit singles. He is very interested in the paranormal and first wrote to me after reading one of my earlier books.

In 1983 Neville saw a UFO. He was setting off to drive to Manchester for a performance when he observed a brilliant egg shape in the sky. It hovered there glinting in the evening sun and did not seem to be attracting much attention. When he reached Manchester, he called home across the Pennines to ask relatives whether there had been any local media stories. There had not. But he is sure of what he saw.

Around the same time the group were rehearsing in a large, old house with a recording studio set-up. On several occasions, as they started their work, a presence manifested in the room. It was always in the vicinity of the microphone. Neville explains: 'The room went cold. It was even cold in the summertime ... Then a ghastly smell seemed to pour through the microphone and went right up my nose and down my throat. Needless to say, I was scared and began to feel sick. I had to retire to the bedroom in order to vomit.'

They checked the area thoroughly. It was a modern building, less than twenty years old. There were no problems with the drains. Although this smell was detected by others, no source for it was ever discovered. Eventually they quit using the building – particularly after the microphone lead began to 'whiplash' all by itself, without anyone's touching it!

Neville suspects that this may have had something to do with him personally. Once, whilst visiting a psychic fayre, he strolled past a medium giving readings and she shouted over, 'Leave, please. Your vibes are so strong they are interfering with my work!' He has on other occasions been told that he is full of power and could be a medium himself. He has also been regularly accused of 'draining energy' from psychic people he meets.

Neville is sincere and baffled. He told me: 'I don't think I'm a Uri Geller, as I can't bend spoons. ... But I do seem to unbalance other psychics. I would like to learn to channel this energy for good use. I have already done some limited psychic healing.'

It is small wonder that Neville is afraid of my using his real name. But it is commendable that this quite serious tussle with strange emotional forces is not being used for public advantage.

I am grateful to those TV performers, employees of TV companies and other people who were very helpful in my quest for information. It would be wrong to imply that I met with or talked in person to all the personalities named in this book, but I was fortunate enough to get the opportunity to do this with quite a few, and I thank them for their kindness and their precious time. Other stories were collected on my safari hunts through the obscure literature of parapsychology, and my meetings with its better proponents.

There is a fair mixture of tales in here, and I would not even attempt to vouch for them all. If the occasional exaggeration or publicist hype has slipped in, I apologize. I tried to avoid them, and I will present the claims as accurately as I can, citing sources where relevant. After that, it is up to you to form your own conclusions about what is, isn't or may be going on.

The 'soap opera' theme is rather loosely applied. Not all the programmes involved in the text fit that genre by any description. Many do, however, so the book's title was justified. In any case, I liked the sound of it, so I did not think it necessary to seek further justification.

Most of the other stories feature actors in popular TV programmes of one kind or another. Although a couple of meaningful diversions are thrown in here and there, there is always a loose TV connection of some sort.

Very possibly you will not recognize all the names that crop up. Some, of course, are very famous and appear in series that are shown the world over. Others may be less well known outside Britain. But I doubt if that matters very much. These are TV people, sharing with you their strange experiences. If they were plumbers or house-wives, you would not know them either. At least you *do* start with the knowledge that they share something in common. And it may be something that offers clues towards an understanding of the paranormal.

Try to bear in mind that it is less the story-teller and more the story that counts. And these stories can be odd – very odd indeed.

Sit back, suspend judgment for a few hours and enjoy the prospect of being astonished.

Episode One: Another World

Stephanie Beacham: A Return from Death

Stephanie Beacham is a British actress, known in the UK for her stage roles and for the highly successful ITV serial Connie. *This had a second series cancelled when the call came from the bright lights of LA. She was then a major hit in what the producer Phil Redmond calls a 'soap bubble', a spin-off from an earlier big budget series:* The Colbys *led Stephanie to* Dynasty *to play the role of a 'super-bitch with a soft centre' and rival to Joan Collins.*

In 1984 Stephanie died. Well, sort of. She had to enter hospital for what was supposed to be a routine operation. She was only thirty-six, but surgery is an invasion of one's body and there is always some risk. Of course, normally that risk is worth the taking – often it *has* to be taken, and it is mostly slight in comparison with the decision not to have your illness treated. After all, nothing will go wrong. That only happens to other people.

For Stephanie things began well, but a problem developed and she drifted into a daze of unconsciousness. It was at this point that the whole event became very bizarre. She saw dim figures around her. She knew they were human but did not recognize them. They seemed to want her to go with them, dragging her towards a beautiful glowing light. It was the most brilliant thing she had ever witnessed, dazzling there in front of her as she drifted across the ether towards it.

Something inside told Stephanie that this was the end, that she was, in fact, dying. But there was a peculiar sense of calmness. Then she observed what looked like an eye, rushing towards her. She was almost being sucked into this vortex.

Inside her mind she now knew the truth. It was not time to die, and she should return. As in a film being wound in reverse, she was tugged back through space and with an imperceptible bump found herself back on her hospital bed, fighting for life.

Struggling desperately, she reached and touched the emergency button, and nursing staff scuttled to her aid. Of course, thankfully, she survived, none the worse for her ordeal and in many respects a great deal better. She was left with a deep conviction that there *is* life after death and that also, if we live on *after* death, it is reasonable to imagine that we may also live *before* we are born.

Stephanie now embraces the tenets of certain Eastern thinking on the question of reincarnation and believes that we can determine how things are going to be, the next time around, by virtue of the deeds we do in this earthly existence. The philosophy is part of Buddhism and is being adopted by a surprising number of actors these days (see Patrick Duffy, p.66). It seems to offer to many a logical way of rationalizing the meaning of life, death and all the baffling bits in between.

However you view this close encounter with death, it had a profound effect on a knowledgeable and intelligent actress. She has no doubts that it seemed real and was real, in some sense or another.

In fact, this is what is termed a 'near death experience' (NDE), and it is being studied in depth by doctors and psychologists.[4] *It has now been claimed by thousands the world over, from different cultures and with many religious beliefs. It shares most of the characteristics described by Stephanie, even down to the 'eye' (variously termed a 'telescope' or, quite commonly, a 'tunnel'). It happens at the point of death in an accident or during surgery, and experts are agreed that* something *is going on, although they are yet to concur as to precisely what this is.*

Some feel the answer must be medical (i.e. exposure to the drugs or anaesthetics), but this does not explain the non-hospital cases in such situations as a car-crash. Others suggest it might be a mechanism by the brain to ease the passage into extinction. However, no one really knows.

The popular American hospital soap St Elsewhere, *rightly awarded for its excellent writing, handled the NDE in an episode of the 1986-7 series, when one of the doctors was shot whilst treating a patient and fought for his life in the operating theatre.*

It utilized many of the details of real NDEs, such as that reported by Stephanie Beacham.

Richard Beckinsale: Greetings From the Other Side

One of the great tragedies of British acting was the loss of Richard Beckinsale through a heart attack at the cruelly young age of thirty-two. He starred in several popular comedy series, from Granada's The Lovers *to the classic* Porridge, *in which he played Ronnie Barker's cell-mate. He was married to actress Judy Loe.*

Whether you believe in survival after death may depend upon a personal experience. But many, including show-business professionals, were at least partially persuaded by the internationally famous medium Doris Stokes, who passed over herself in May 1987 after giving many star sittings.

The family of Richard Beckinsale were part of that collection, because the jovial actor 'returned' on a number of occasions to Doris with messages for her to pass on.

These tended to occur when Doris was in Nottingham, his home town, giving one of her performances. She reported one session in detail, stating that Richard had explained how he had just returned from the USA, where he had travelled in spirit to accompany a member of the family. That a relative had been travelling in the States was later confirmed by his parents, Margaret and Arthur Beckinsale, who added that Doris's other message, reputedly direct from Richard, also made sense.

She had, for example, told how Mrs Beckinsale had that day been for a hospital check-up and been pronounced fit. Richard also wanted it to be known that he had always yearned to be a musician and was finally getting his wish on the other side. In true generosity he gave a little note to pass on to Judy Loe, telling her how pleased he was at her finding happiness with someone new.

Everything was said to fit in precisely with Richard's

character and how he might have been expected to behave.

The trouble with stories like this is that they are personally meaningful but offer very little in the way of conviction for anyone else.

I am sure that the Beckinsales were genuinely impressed, and I have no reason to question the sincerity of Mrs Stokes, but the problem comes in deciding whether the medium could obtain the information by normal means.

By this I do not imply cheating – although that is always going to be a suspicion in some people's eyes when you are dealing with well-known celebrities whose life-stories are easily accessible. Rather, I am suggesting that, if there is such a thing as ESP, a medium might be able to read the mind of the family member who is present and, even without realizing it take in relevant ideas and yet assume the message came from the deceased.

After all, if that message is understood, the information offered was known to the sitter, and if it was known, it could have come from his or her mind in the first place. (See Stokes and Dearsley, A Host of Voices, *Futura, 1984.)*

Michael Bentine: Not Just Gooning Around

Michael was an intelligence officer with an RAF bomber wing during the war and went on to become one of the founder members of radio and TV's world-famous 'Goons'. His zany humour has developed into a number of programmes in the decades since, many of which were specially designed for children. I particularly recall It's A Square World *from my schooldays, with its brilliant animated models that acted out long, amusing sequences. More recently, he has been a mainstay of series such as* Potty Time *and* Madabout. *Yet, as so often with comedians, the laughter masks great inner sadness and despair in his life. A son was killed in an air crash, a daughter taken from his family through illness.*

Despite such horrendous tests of his strength and character, he has seen them through with much bravery and composure. Michael has never failed in his primary directive – to entertain and amuse. It is, he says, why he was put on this earth. But there are other reasons why Michael Bentine has been able to overcome the tragic obstacles that have littered his life. He holds a deep conviction about the meaning and purpose of existence: that life does not end when you die but, in many real senses, opens up to a whole new vista of awareness and of possibilities.

In biography listings Michael calls himself a writer, actor, comedian and parapsychologist. Of all the TV celebrities I have met, he is the one who most openly acknowledges the paranormal in his life. He does so from a standpoint of personal experiences but also by virtue of his extensive understanding and knowledge.

I have met him twice. Once we did a BBC late-night radio show in Manchester together. This was 1975, and I had every reason to recall it, because it was my first. He had no special reason to remember, but his phenomenal recollection, or his pleasant charm, indicated that he did.

The BBC in Leeds were kind enough to allow me to conduct this interview with him, after he had appeared on a show there. What struck me the most, aside from his very genuine and friendly nature, was his exceptional comprehension of parapsychology, the serious study of strange phenomena. I was not talking with someone who has just had a few strange experiences which have piqued their interest. I was talking to one of the most astute of Britain's thinkers and researchers in this subject.

To combine that with his professional career takes a special kind of magic, particularly when you remember the prejudice that still exists against the unknown. I have often met folk in high-profile occupations who are terrified of speaking out about their own beliefs. They fear that they will suffer a loss of prestige, may even take irrevocable sidesteps away from promotion, and I have to say that these are not always paranoid delusions. I have seen it happen to people who deserved much better and were owed sympathy and understanding which they never got.

In a sense, Michael Bentine speaks for all of them, by his fortitude and insistence that he does not hide behind the cameras or use public life as an excuse. Because he tells it as it really is and of how he sincerely feels, he offers encouragement to many others without the same opportunity.

In two factual books about the paranormal, he has expressed his attitude toward mediumship and how he came to be introduced to such sensitive subjects by his Peruvian father.[5] He does not shirk from pointing out that during his father's 'investigation of the supernatural', he (Michael) came into contact with many frauds and tricksters, quickly learning to tell the difference.

Because of the battles of his daughter against cancer, he has also come to embrace the tenets of psychic healing. It is very interesting to note how the public's impression of the medium as a money-grabbing, PR-chasing showman (or more often show-woman) masks the truth that most mediums do it for nothing and prefer to channel their energy into attempts to heal others.

Since Michael began to awaken his abilities when still a child, I was curious about how at that age he could distinguish between clairvoyance and imagination, with which many youngsters are very gifted.

'I don't think children really differentiate between the two,' he remarked. 'I've always been cursed – or gifted, whichever you like – with a vivid imagination. I see things in pictures and I can almost hear words sometimes. ... I think I do hear them. And at other times I just get a sense of emotion ... a sense of atmosphere. ... "Get out of this place, it's not for you!" ... a sense of evil, or a sense of peace. It is essentially the reaction of an artist's mind.'

This intrigued me, because it seems so close to my impression of why actors are so frequently tied in with the paranormal. They can absorb the emotions of a circumstance and, as Michael says, use artistic talent to turn them into picture form.

That really *is* clairvoyance. But where do you draw the line with imagination? Perhaps as children grow and lose this talent, because the hard practicalities of the world are taught them as more important, they may gain reality at the expense of something equally precious.

Michael had learnt how to paint from his elder brother. I have often noted how common it is to find regular experients of the paranormal to be creatively gifted in some way such as this. You may notice it only in their handwriting, full of curls and neatness, or it shines from their soul in more obvious fashion by virtue of what they enjoy most – art, poetry, writing etc.

Indeed, Michael pointed out that he always knew that, 'I had something which other children also had, but only in embryo, whereas mine was being developed because of my father's interest in these things.' But *all* children possess the potential; of this he is certain. He reminded me how, during a half-day holiday, any young mind can go to the local stream and pretend it is the Amazon and it will *be* the Amazon.

He pointed out that some children naturally have visual imagination and others auditory or tactile (i.e. brought on by hearing or touch), particularly a child blind from birth. Of these, he says in explanation, 'Very often he has a vivid imagination, and yet he has never *seen* anything.'

But this only made my question more pertinent. How could you tell the difference between imagination, inspiration and clairvoyance if they are so similar?

Immediately he returned: 'I think they're all exactly the same. Someone will say to me (in an effort to dismiss my experiences), "Don't you understand? It's just your imagination" – and I say, "Of course, it is. Now let me see … where do you buy this? Do you buy it by the kilogram or the pint?" I don't know what they mean. Such questions suggest that they have no imagination themselves. If they did, they would realize that imagination is the ability to create images or integrate images from memory or impressions you have received. Even smells or the feel of wind in your face can conjure up images. All sorts of things. And when you do this, you *are* an artist.'

Michael has had numerous personal experiences which have convinced him many times over of the reality of the paranormal.

During World War II, for example, whilst he was an intelligence officer in command of a Polish unit of bomber pilots conducting raids from Britain, he came into close contact with UFOs. His crew returned from a raid on

Peenemunde and described strange balls of pulsating light that were floating beside them. They believed them to be some sort of weapon, so Michael debriefed the airmen and asked, 'What did they do to you?' They said, 'Nothing', so he said (chuckling), 'It's not a very effective weapon, is it?'

But later he found that the Americans were investigating stories from their own bomber crews during late 1944 and into 1945. They called the things 'foo fighters' (from a US comic strip where 'foo' meant 'fire'). Something strange really was flying about.

He has since had other experiences of glowing things in the sky and developed a personal interest. Indeed, he once played the UFO 'expert' to Patrick Moore's UFO disbeliever on an edition of Patrick's long-running BBC TV show *The Sky at Night* when the topic was debated. Michael argued persuasively in favour of the existence of the phenomenon.

One of his many premonitions turned out to be rather disturbing. He was in the south Midlands doing a performance at a hotel owned by Danny La Rue. The audience was from a local factory. He retired upstairs after what he said was a fun show – although, 'You can't get much more basic than doing an hour in front of a lot of diesel engineers. It's not the most spiritual experience in the world.' He paused for a grin at the memory, then became more reserved as he recalled what happened upon his entering his bedroom: 'A voice said as clear as a bell in my ear – "Blood sacrifice". I shot the light on. Nobody there. So I put it out again and the same thing – "Blood sacrifice".'

At the time his youngest daughter was due to fly out to Africa and, having already lost his son in an air crash, he was naturally concerned. So he pleaded into the night that he did not want to know about this and tried to block out the mental image. But it kept recurring all night, and he got no sleep.

In the morning he asked the manager if the building had a reputation for being haunted, but no such story was known. However, it was built on an old Saxon burial-ground, and the hotelier suggested that Michael might be picking up something from far back in the past.

The day continued, dull, miserable and with ceaseless rain. He did the second (and final) night's show and returned to the bedroom. Exactly the same message boomed into his head. So, in utter desperation, he phoned home and received the welcome news that his wife had just spoken with their daughter, who had landed safely at her destination.

Relieved, he set off home and had reached Woodstock in Oxfordshire when the voice in his mind began again. So he stopped the car, got out and said, 'Look – I don't want to know about this nonsense.' And it stopped. 'So I drove, very, very carefully, back to London, arrived at my home in Esher and got out. My wife said, "What's wrong?", because I must have looked ashen. I told of my extraordinary experience and said, "I don't like it." She went and made a cup of tea – the universal remedy – and I sat down to drink it. The phone bell rang, she answered and came back to tell me. "Your friend Airey Neave has been blown up at the Houses of Parliament. His car has been blown to bits. They're sure it's him." '

The call had been from Scotland Yard. In 1979 the Conservative minister had been horribly killed in a car-bomb attack by the IRA – one of their most audacious strikes in mainland Britain. Whilst Michael had no political ties with him, he had been Neave's MI9 pupil during the war. They were currently working together on new air-safety regulations, and the call from the police had been to warn Michael to check his own vehicle, just in case someone had extended vengeance to any of Airey Neave's colleagues.

Fortunately everything was fine, but as Michael sat down to take all this in, he heard another voice in his mind, giving a quotation from *Pilgrim's Progress* – which he had not heard or thought of in many years. The words were: 'And all the trumpets sounded for him on the other side.'

Some days later he sat in St Martin's-in-the-Field, attending Airey Neave's memorial service. Prime Minister Margaret Thatcher spoke the eulogy, with the words, 'And all the trumpets sounded for him on the other side.'

But what was the point of this two-day warning? It was

not sufficiently specific to be of any help in preventing the tragedy. Michael says: 'I was picking up a probability factor. If you accept the implication that you survive the death change, the chances are that you can see something that is likely to happen, and search round for a way to warn them. Perhaps I picked it up because I was then associated with Neave. I just don't know.'

However, it is not always an event with which he has a personal link. In Spain, during a pleasant break on a sunny day, having just done some writing for one of his many books, Michael suddenly got a picture, 'on my inner screen', of '... a five- or six-storey building, barbed wire around the wall, helicopters appearing overhead ... and I thought, "What the heck's going on?". I saw two single-decker buses crash into the gates of what was obviously a compound. And I thought, "My God! I'm picking up an attempt to rescue the hostages in Iran." '

This was the time (autumn, 1980) when a group of Americans had been held captive for many months and President Carter was desperate to find a way to free them before he left office. But the existence of such a daring and (as it transpired) foolhardy plan to get them out was naturally shrouded in ultra-tight secrecy, for very obvious and necessary reasons.

Aside from these visual images, Michael Bentine also had a sense of aircraft some miles away in the desert which he knew to be C-135 Hercules troop-transporters. Also one word kept repeating inside his mind: 'Failure! Failure! Failure!'

His impression was that, having trained in intelligence planning and being familiar with exactly this sort of operation, he was amenable to the news. 'Because I am in a relaxed state of mind, perhaps someone is transmitting and I'm receiving,' he pondered. Going indoors, he switched on the radio, but the news carried no reports. So he knew the rescue mission had not actually happened, and began to suspect it was a warning and he might be able to prevent the terrible disaster that would follow if it did fail.

'I have a couple of friends in the House [of Commons] in various parties, so I said, "I am going to ring them."

And my wife said, "Don't be ridiculous. There's an English-speaking phone-operator; it's just a tiny village; the minute you start speaking to our local MP about this, they'll be round here with a police car!'

Thwarted by this logic, he took another course. 'Really to ease my conscience, I wrote an express letter. And I got a letter back about six or seven days later, by which time [the raid] had happened. It was on House of Commons notepaper from my MP friend and said, "My dear Michael, what a remarkable coincidence." ' He had to be cautious, Michael explained to me with a cynical smile. But the MP had added 'Of course, you didn't get it all right. You went wrong on the buses –' I thought, "Yes, I did." '

The aborted raid was doomed to disaster because of a catalogue of errors involving the C-135s and the helicopters. No buses had stormed the gates, but the mission had indeed been a catastrophic failure.

Michael Bentine told the story in one of his books. On a tour in the USA, he was introduced to a man with the CIA who had read the book. He said: 'We're terribly interested in that business about your picking up the raid.'

'I explained that I had probably tuned into a worried officer on the ship sailing to the Middle East and going over the thing in his mind, thinking it was all going to go wrong. But I reminded him that I didn't get it *all* right, you know. And the CIA man said, "Oh yes, you did. The plan was for two buses to crash into the gate at the same time as the rest of it happened." That, of course, had *not* been publicized.'

As Michael emphatically argues: 'All that was documented *before* it happened, so it could be coincidence, but why, when you are sitting in a garden of a tiny villa in Spain, would you pick up such an extraordinary event?'

Other personal messages, including ones obtained from his dead son, have suggested to Michael Bentine that we do survive death. I asked him how he could justify such an amazing concept as life after death. 'It's very simple,' he said, with typical laughter. 'You cannot destroy energy. It's a scientific fact. There's nothing complex about that.'

He offered me a question: 'Take the individual or

personality – the thing that you love in someone. Does that survive? I mean, if you love somebody and they lose a leg, do you automatically love them one quarter less? Of course you don't. It's the personality that you love, or hate, or dislike, or feel totally neutral about. That is what lives on in your memory or, perhaps, as an extant individual field. I don't know, and I don't think anyone knows an answer to that question.'

Michael Bentine has grown beyond the stage of belief or disbelief in the paranormal. Too many things have happened to him. He is now far more concerned with understanding it and helping others to appreciate its potential. Whilst he considers it a force that can be used for good or evil, he responded firmly to my suggestion that this surely meant it was dangerous to promote a wider acceptance of psychic abilities.

'Let's face it,' he insisted. 'Electricity can be used for good or evil. It's a question of how you, the human being, *use* the power. A Tibetan lama once told a great friend of mine (a psychologist and physicist) something I think was very wise. He said: "All the angels and all the devils are inside ourselves, and it is up to us how they manifest." You can use explosives to blast precious ore out of a hillside or you can use it to blast people apart. Explosive itself is not dangerous.'

Of course, the real problem comes in removing the paranormal from its image of seance rooms and occult magic tricks. Books on the subject end up on the shelves alongside tea-leaf-reading and philosophies of ancient Atlanteans, yet they are about human experiences, just as books about psychology or personal battles against illness, or brave deeds and biographical stories are about human experiences.

How do we overcome that? Michael had a suggestion for genuine enquirers: 'It goes back to a very simple piece of advice – "Seek and ye shall find." But seek with a certain amount of rationale behind you. Don't just go around and believe everything that everybody tells you or that's written in books.'

He considers that it will be very difficult to prove the reality of the paranormal to the satisfaction of science, because too many scientists are merely technologists, tethered to their machinery – and not truly creative thinkers.

'You cannot conduct a series of repeatable, empiric experiments with a living being, because the being keeps changing.' He took a sip of BBC tea. 'For example, I only have to drink this cup of tea and my whole chemical balance alters. I only have to go to the loo and instantly it's changed again. You cannot have a repeatable experiment unless you repeat every facet of the conditions with which you set the experiment up.'

Another problem he envisages is this: 'How can you analyse a masterpiece? You can sit down and study music and say, "Ah well, it went 'ping' followed by 'pong', so every time you get a 'ping' followed by a 'pong' you're going to get a masterpiece." But that's not the way it happens.'

To Michael Bentine, the paranormal is an art of human imagination or intuition, and science has no way of explaining any art, except in dry, mechanical terms. This does nothing to describe what differentiates good art from bad art, 'To me, it's that spark of creativity, something that is essential in man and not, say, in a machine. That is the difference. All this talk by scientists of "Oh, it doesn't show up on my machine or my instruments." They forget what is important. Which came first, the instrument or the man who invented it? And to invent it he had to imagine it.'

That act of imagination would not, of course, be recordable on any instrument ever invented. 'There's the rub,' as they say.

He showed me how he deals rigorously with the many debunkers who set themselves up as protectors of the dogma of rationality. They take every chance to denigrate the paranormal. One said to him, 'You're obviously self-deluded.' So Michael asked him, 'From what omniscient point of view, from what God-like status, do you make such a statement, without knowing the man or examining him? No physician would make a diagnosis of even the most simple malfunction of the body without a considerably closer study than that. The trouble is, there are too many self-confessed geniuses in this world.'

Instead of deathly dull experiments inside a laboratory to prove or disprove ESP, Michael Bentine prefers to research the paranormal by teaching children. 'They don't have the doubt syndrome,' he notes. You don't need to waste time re-educating them that such a thing just *might* be possible, because they have not yet unlearnt the probability that it is!

He has worked a good deal on the subject of dowsing, which he thinks is a perfectly natural ability that everyone can be trained to develop. Many so-called 'primitive' cultures use it as a common method of finding water, perhaps allowing a twig or stick to magnify little motions in the body triggered by the subconscious mind when it *knows* water is nearby. Michael believes it operates because '... we are made of the earth and, therefore, we can tune in and use our natural antennae.'

This is no mystical thing in his estimation. 'I've taught over a hundred children to dowse. It's easy. I have a whole gaggle of them in Peru doing it. They belong to a Catholic college, so if it was anything mystical, I don't think the principal would have been too happy.'

In one experiment with Thames TV, the film crew buried a hosepipe underground at a nursery near Reading. It was quite invisible and undetectable by normal means. Michael spent a few minutes training four ten-year-olds to dowse. Two girls and one boy then did this and placed little stick windmills to mark where they believed the serpent-like outline of the buried hose would be. The pipe was then dug up, and it displaced every single marker as it came out precisely where the three children had gauged.

But one boy had acted alone and done something quite different. He had laid his windmills in one straight line, well away from the hose. Afterwards, Michael congratulated the team on the success of the experiment, but he told the nursery manager that he was disappointed that one of the boys had got it so far wrong. The man looked at Michael with amused surprise and said, 'What do you mean? He marked the water main!'

To Michael Bentine, this is the way to progress. That is

how these things will come to be accepted as normal, not paranormal.

I could see him winding up for one of his stories, with the familiar grin and chortle. He told me: 'Where it all goes wrong is when researchers say this.' He proceeded, after adopting a mock scientific accent: 'You know it's worrying. We had a rectal microphone and wires halfway up this so-called psychic's nostrils. We had seventeen EEG machines attached to him, and do you know, he couldn't perform at all.'

Michael looked at me, returned to his normal voice and said: 'I wonder how well Yehudi Menuhin would play his violin or Sir Laurence Olivier give a performance under those conditions? It is essentially a personal ability of the individual that you are investigating. So I think we must ask people who wish to investigate these matters to keep their minds open, because, if they shut them firmly, they are just technologists. They are failing to live up to Albert Einstein's wonderful maxim, which I always keep in front of me. He said, "Imagination is more valuable than knowledge, because it increases the sum of human knowledge by that one new idea." '

We swopped notes about scientists who were sticking their necks out and braving the loss of research grants in order to take on board the paranormal. We had both worked with and applauded people like the great engineers Professors Arthur Ellison and Eric Laithwaite. I told him of a seminar on 'Science and ESP' which I had been invited to take part in and which had been organized by a psychologist at Manchester University. And he smiled when I mentioned an interview I had just carried out with Ray Leonard, a professor of computers who was so interested in the paranormal that he was writing serious novels about the subject.

Professor Leonard is head of the Total Technology unit at the University of Manchester Institute of Science and Technology, I remarked. Michael beamed at me with delight, grinning and chuckling: 'What a wonderful name! But who can be head of total technology? Surely it has to be God?'

We ended on a serious note. He nodded his approval that these changes were occurring. Entertainer that he is,

Michael Bentine gave a good demonstration that he is also a very deep and serious thinker about the problems that the planet may face. Whether or not the paranormal can solve these difficulties, we cannot know, but it might help.

He added sombrely: 'I am glad there are scientists with imagination, because, if we continue in the material way which we have been in the past, we are not going to be here too long.'

Amanda Burton: The Luck of the Irish

Amanda was one of the original stars of Channel 4's upmarket soap opera Brookside *(see also Doreen Sloane). From 1982 to 1987 she played Heather Haversham, a young, independent Irishwoman with a troubled love-life. It was her first major role after studying at Manchester Polytechnic, living in my home town of Stockport and working in theatre at Bolton. Shortly before she joined the Liverpool soap, we 'worked together' when I made a film for the aborted Granada TV series* Mersey Pirate, *which was to be Amanda's first short-lived foray into television. Since leaving* Brookside, *she is now a co-star in* Boon, *the ITV saga of an urban cowboy.*

Amanda has quite a pedigree. She is related, via her grandmother, to the legendary Oscar Wilde and was raised in strife-torn Londonderry, with a very early and painful marriage to show. In some respects, her life mirrored that of her character in *Brookside*.

Perhaps because of her Irish upbringing, she has her fair share of superstitious associations. Of course, these are often a way of life to an actor, but Amanda seems particularly keen on them. She is said not to want to look at the new moon through glass and never fails to observe the peculiar British tradition of repeating the words 'White rabbits', three times, as each new month dawns. But, own up, how many of you do the same?

However, Amanda seems to have developed these things into an acute kind of sensitivity. She reports that on many occasions she has had the experience of thinking about someone whom she has not seen in many months and almost immediately they turn up on her doorstep. On the one level she sees this as strange, but it is such a commonplace factor in her life that she has rather come to take it for granted.

This ability of Amanda Burton's is nothing extraordinary. Many people appear to possess it at a low level and call it intuition. Something inside senses the coming event, and the thought bubbles up through the layers of awareness to appear as a feeling, or gut reaction, or perhaps the realization that you are thinking of someone, but you do not know why.

To some it may be no more than coincidence (for example, when you hum a tune and then switch the radio on to find it is playing). But others say it is the simplest form of psychic experience that exists – so simple, in fact, that almost everyone has it at one time or another, and so it tends to be considered not paranormal at all.

Johnny Caesar: Is There a Doctor in the House?

Emmerdale Farm is a soap that has been growing in popularity since it was started by Yorkshire TV in the early seventies. In 1988 it acquired a new peak-viewing schedule on a national basis and expanded its audience to almost 12 million in Britain alone.

Part of the rural community of the fictional Beckindale is the Geordie who works for the large estate. A cheerful chap and dairyman with family troubles, he is noted for his impenetrable accent and wellies. His role has developed in recent years, but this spell as a TV personality was presaged by many years on the road, 'Treading the boards' is the expression that actors use, and Johnny Caesar has done that regularly for a quarter of a century. The archetypal 'Johnny of all trades', he was singer, musician, performer, comedian and character actor, all rolled into one, before settling for the more sedate life (and steady income) that Emmerdale Farm *can offer. But it was whilst enjoying those years on the road, touring virtually every city and theatre in Britain, that the paranormal began to take hold of his life and change him in many ways, as he put it, '... from a complete sceptic and non-believer into someone who* knows *that there is something going on'.*

Johnny is now settled in a happy family life in Derbyshire, but it was not always like that. From 1963 he began to know the stresses and strains of perpetual touring: a different town or city every week, finding 'digs' to stay in where he was plied with food by ever-helpful landladies, plus, of course, the sheer exhilaration and terror of facing a new audience.

Would this be the night when he stormed the show and attracted the famous producer sitting unannounced in the theatre? Or would it be one of those rare but awful experiences where things just don't go right and, as the saying goes, the actor 'dies'?

On 28 February 1970 the latter was to happen, only this time it was not in a theatrical or metaphorical sense. Johnny Caesar really did die, in a literal manner!

He was playing a show at an hotel in Aviemore, Scotland. The popular ski resort has many attractions in mid winter. Somehow a February night on a stage in some industrial city seems far colder than one amidst the warmth, hospitality and beautiful mountain scenery of the Highlands.

Johnny was at the part of his act where he played his guitar and sang but, with someone who is noted for comedy, the audience always expects the unexpected, so when there was a flash and muffled bang, and the strings burst into sizzling flames, ripples of laughter began. As Johnny crashed to the floor, letting his precious guitar smash uncontrollably beside him, everyone still chuckled. After all, it was just a part of the act. But why was he staying there, silent and paralysed? Surely no further mirth could be milked from this scene? It was time to get up and get on with the show.

But Johnny was not getting up. The crowd saw that now. He was really in trouble. He was prone on the ground and showing no signs of life. The chuckles were cut short and were replaced by anguish. This had been no joke. The performer was in desperate trouble.

Johnny said to me: 'I knew that I had been electrocuted.

I could not breathe. I was stuck there firm upon the stage floor. But my mind was alert. I was able to think about everything clearly. I told myself, "At least I have a minute or so to live. I'm dying, but it's not instantaneous. I'm still here. Surely somebody will realize what is wrong and save me." '

Around him colleagues at the hotel were gathering their wits. They could see that this was serious. The cry was uttered, 'Is there a doctor in the house?' – the corny line from so many bad movies. This time it was spoken for real. And on its answer the fate of a young man would depend.

With good fortune, the answer to the question was 'Yes.' The doctor raced forward as soon as he saw the danger. His training and compassion immediately took hold, and he reacted instinctively. Seconds could mean the difference between life and death. He thumped Johnny on the chest.

Meanwhile, Johnny Caesar was observing all this with a curious sense of detachment. He knew what was happening, but it was almost as if it were taking place on TV, in some hospital drama series. There was no real sense of personal urgency, no pain or suffering.

He told me: 'I tried to get up, but I felt tired. There was no hurt involved. In fact, it felt very nice. It was a lovely, warm sensation just lying there. I almost think I *wanted* to die. Or, more probably, it seemed the simplest thing to do. I had this weird thought that the easiest, most pleasant and least painful outcome would be to slip away. I just knew it would be a lot harder to come back than to stay.'

Whilst he had no idea at the time, Johnny was undergoing the classic 'near death experience' (NDE) that we met in connection with Stephanie Beacham. In 1970 this was something generally unknown to the public. The book *Life After Life* by investigating psychiatrist Ron Moody, reporting on cases he had met in his work, was still some years from publication.[6] Until it came along, very few knew that such things took place.

But Johnny did. For him, it was all too real. As the doctor worked away, struggling to get his heart beating again, he was now drifting, entering the second phase of the experience. He was going out of his body.

'I felt myself go out,' he remembers. 'I just sort of drifted up. There was still no pain. It was really nice and peaceful. I was fluttering like I was a bird on the wing. There I was, just above myself, looking down, and I could actually see me down there. See my body being worked on. See them trying to bring me back to life.'

As is typical of this experience, Johnny was detached from what was happening. But then a sense of purpose – a sense of life itself – came back, and he began to understand the situation. 'I thought to myself, "I don't like this." I have to go back down there. So I did. Just like that, I did it. I was back in my body and feeling what was happening, but in a dazed sort of way.'

But with the return there was a trade-off. Johnny's heart had stopped for 1½ minutes. Now it was beating again, and it hurt. He had also suffered serious burns. He was rushed to hospital, where he took weeks to recover and months to get back to work. But he had survived. He had come back from death.

Clinical definitions of where life stops are very hard to come by, but if one relies upon the functioning of the heart, he was certainly well on his way to the other side. Since his brain was still lucid, it might be argued that he was really in a 'limbo' state which is not the same as true death. But it is comforting to know that Johnny's account of what took place is precisely like so many others from all over the world. Even if it is the ultimate hallucination, we should all learn to accept that death is something never to be afraid of. If all that occurs is one last desperate throw by the body's defence systems, removing pain and fear as we fade forever, at least we should understand that the act of death is far from unpleasant. In no sense is it something to terrify us.

We must wonder if the same process occurs to all those who don't pull through as Johnny did. We know that in some cases the events seem to go further. People who have 'died' for much longer say they drift into another realm, a friendly, ethereal land. This may just be a place of dreams that is snuffed out forever when the brain cells die and death becomes irretrievable, but it does not refute the possibility that we survive into another state. Indeed, the fact that we appear to survive the first stages of the death process implies that it may actually be likely that we survive beyond that. Otherwise, why bother with this elaborate method of detachment, painlessness, drifting out of the body and hallucination? Surely it would be simpler if we were just rendered instantly unconscious, where death could swiftly overcome us?

And those sceptics who claim that these out-of-body or near-death experiences are the product of hospital drugs that alter the state of consciousness should ponder on Johnny's story (which is far from unique). It refutes that possibility beyond any question.

Johnny Caesar was on no drugs when these things happened to him. Whatever caused the experience was a very natural act, and a consequence of being human and in dire peril.

He battled through this crisis and returned to the life he loved. However, this terrible shock to the system had left an eerie sort of invisible mark. In subtle ways it had changed him inside.

In August that same year, Johnny had just returned to work. He was to perform at a club near Porthcawl in South Wales during week nights. He had been recuperating in Newcastle, so the new job and new challenge required a drive of 400 miles on the Sunday, for first he had to go to a working men's club in Swansea.

At the club, after the show, Johnny was inevitably exhausted. Someone from Porthcawl was due to meet him there and lead him down to the accommodation that was booked, but the man never turned up, so the drummer in the band made a suggestion. He had an antique shop in town, with a flat above. He kindly offered this to Johnny for the entire week. Porthcawl is twenty miles down the coast from Swansea, so Johnny had to decline the long-term option, but he was grateful for a bed on that particular night, without having to face more miles on this already lengthy day.

The room was evidently not prepared for a sleeping guest. It was piled high with old things for the shop – pots, pans, pictures of the Crimean War, and a huge brass bed.

'Sorry it isn't up to much,' his friend apologized, but Johnny waved him away, explaining that it would be a lot more comfortable than sleeping in the car. 'Oh, by the way,' the drummer added, 'if you hear any noises in the night, don't panic. There are flats above this one that are occupied. It will just be people in there.'

There was no lock on the door, so Johnny jammed a chair up against it. He tried to flip through a book which he'd brought to read but was extremely tired and needed sleep. He was doing something he had done a thousand times before during his years on the road: facing a one-off night in a strange room and new bed, without the comforts of home.

But tonight he could sleep practically anywhere. He flicked off the light switch and barely noticed that there was only one tiny window letting in a chink of light from the street outside. Around him the assorted oddments made strange shapes and silhouette shadows, but this was all lost on him, for Johnny had only one thought in mind – to put the rigours of the day behind him and get to sleep. He tumbled easily and quickly into dreamless slumber. Then he awoke suddenly.

'It was one of those moments when you are instantly awake,' Johnny explained. 'I was lying there on my left side. There was no dreaminess. Everything was in sharp focus. And I had been disturbed because somebody was attempting to get in bed with me. I could see the white jockey shorts. I could tell it was a man.'

Naturally, his first thought was that someone had entered the room by mistake, perhaps a resident from the upstairs flats. But then how had they got in through the door? Fear gripped hold.

Fighting off the terror, Johnny sought to calm himself. There would be a simple explanation. All he had to do was talk to the man and the matter would be resolved. He opened his mouth and started to speak. As he did so, the figure began to fade away. 'It did not disappear immediately. It just seemed to fade away. I was scared out of my wits. Absolutely petrified.'

One thought invaded Johnny's mind: to switch the light on. But to do so required movement out of bed. Nothing he could do would force him to stir. His muscles were locked rigid.

'I'll just pretend it never happened,' he told himself. The

idea echoed in his mind like a litany. He tried to breathe deeply and slowly, forcing calmness into himself.

It took a long time for sleep to overcome him, but eventually it must have done, because later he woke again. Something else had disturbed him. There was a sound coming from over by the door. The handle was turning, and the chair that had been jammed up against it was moving. There could be no doubt about this. Someone – or something – was trying to get into the room.

The nightmare had returned. All the memories of the past few minutes (or was it hours?) had come back. But this time he managed to speak. Johnny called to the force at the other side of the door, and the force responded.

It was a man from one of the other flats. He had left a book in the room, which he had assumed was still empty. All he had been trying to do was come in and get it.

In the morning Johnny took stock of the situation. It had been real. He had no doubt that a man had climbed into his bed, a man who could not have got into the room, a man who was not alive, because he had disappeared into thin air.

'How could you talk about this?' he asked me. 'Everyone would think it was a joke if I said I had slept with a male ghost. But it was no joke. It happened.'

In fact, more than that, Johnny realized now that he had *recognized* the figure. 'It looked exactly like a friend of mine who had committed suicide.'

The victim had been an intelligent and professional man. His suicide bid had been carried out in the open, in front of many witnesses. They had seen it but had not tried to stop it. Instead they had run to tell others. By the time anyone understood what was going on, it was too late.

'It was a cry for help,' Johnny recalled. 'I am sure it was. A cry for help that just went wrong.'

The return of his friend in this mysterious way deeply affected Johnny, but he tried to forget. He had to get on with his career. He had cancelled a season on the isle of Jersey, thanks to the terrible accident at Aviemore, but his chance came again for dates in summer 1971, and this time he took it eagerly.

On Jersey he had the comfort of the friendship of two people from the north-east, a singer called Julie Dawn and her husband, Billy Fontaine. Their time together during that summer was precious, and it was sad to have to split and go their separate ways as the season ended in October – this was particularly so as Johnny had no real permanent home at the time and was living out of a suitcase. For that reason he was more than happy to engineer a reunion with Julie and Billy. In January 1972 he visited them at their home in County Durham. It was everything a meeting with friends ought to be. But it was something extra too: it was to prove a major surprise.

Johnny was in his room. Downstairs they were innocently toying with a ouija board. In the early 1970s the game-manufacturers Waddingtons had put one onto the mass market, despite outcries from some Church authorities. Attempting to contact spirits was blasphemy, they insisted. Doing so in the form of a game, where you moved a plastic pointer around a set of letters on a board, was both silly and dangerous. The critics made their case, but thousands still bought the ouija game and used it in frivolous and not so frivolous efforts to obtain a message from the other side.

Johnny was having nothing to do with this – not until Julie knocked on his door and said: 'Hey, come and see. We've got a message.' She then gave the name and address of a certain north-east road, and Johnny's heart began its thumping once again.

It was a house in which, years before, Johnny himself had lived.

'I was absolutely astonished,' the actor told me. 'I could not believe it. What made it so very impressive was the number they quoted. They could have known that I had lived at that house, but they would only have known it by the number it occupied in recent years. There is no way they could have known the truth.'

He explained what he meant: 'During the war, some of the houses in the road had been bombed. When they were cleared away, this left a gap. Up until the early fifties the situation remained the same. Building-materials were in short supply and there was such a lot of work to do. So the old numbers stayed. The number of my house was then the one that the ouija board had given. But then they rebuilt houses in the gap and had to renumber the entire street. The only number Julie and Billy would have known was this new one. It had been in force for twenty years.'

Intrigued and not a little perturbed by this revelation, Johnny immediately went downstairs to the impromptu seance. The board was continuing to spell out its message, which it insisted was 'for John'. The letters proclaimed that it came from someone with the name of Peter (a pseudonym).

This was the man who had committed suicide.

Here is part of the 'conversation' that ensued. (Q = question by Johnny. P = answer given by the board.)

Q: Have you tried to contact me before?
P: Yes, Swansea.
Q: Why contact me?
P: Now there is a way.
Q: How?
P: Death.
Q: Whose?
P: Yours.
Q: When?
P: 1970.
Q: Was your death an accident?
P: Yes.

Johnny interpreted this as meaning that the electric shock which had temporarily 'killed' him had opened up some kind of channel which then allowed the ghost of his friend to 'come through'.

The astonished performer said to me: 'I now knew in myself that I could do these things, that I had the ability inside me to make contact. This experience in Durham was the thing that really convinced me. There was no other explanation.'

Since these events, Johnny Caesar's outlook on the world has altered markedly. He has also continued to be in tune with the paranormal.

'I can go into a room and get responses,' he confirmed,

'but I don't have the time to develop it. I've studied some books about mediums, like those by Doris Stokes. Perhaps they just use ESP to get their information. They read the atmosphere like I read their books. They might not even realize that this is what they are doing.'

His philosophy on life has changed too: 'I am not frightened by death now. I am frightened only of the sadness it brings to others who are left behind. I tried to tell Peter's mother, but I could not explain it all. I just said that he had come to me and explained it was an accident. She said that she always knew that somehow.'

He smiled. 'You know, I was the original doubting Thomas. But now I've seen it, I have to believe it. I think it's in all of us to believe and look at the comfort that such knowledge can provide for all those who have lost a loved one. Yet, whilst it is exciting in a way, it also seems rather pointless. If a ghost could give us a cure for cancer, there might be a purpose. As it is, having such an experience is like jumping out of a plane with a parachute, without knowing whether it is going to open or not.' (In other words, if ghosts could impart information unknown to anyone on earth, their purpose in coming back would be justified. So often, it seems, ghosts say things the living already know.)

His encounters with the supernatural have continued. 'I lived with a girl for ten days in 1976,' he grinned. 'But it's all right. She was a ghost.'

At the time he had been in a room right next to the theatre in Paignton, Devon, where he was performing. 'The bedroom was always cold. There would be a little flash of light across the room too. When it happened, I used to say into the empty air, "Do you mind? You're frightening me." '

Johnny saw this ghost just once. It was a girl wearing a cap who seemed to be dressed as a cleaner. 'She sat on the edge of the bed and spoke to me – or into my mind, at least. I wasn't frightened, because I have never heard of a ghost hurting anybody. It's fascinating really, and the only fear that comes is the fear of the unknown that we all seem to have.'

During that stay in Paignton he had a lot of props to use

on stage. Before going on, he had a ritual which saw him speak out loud all the things he was to take with him, to double-check he had forgotten nothing.

One night he began the check: 'Guns located … Got hat … Guitars in tune … Don't leave me … Got wigs.'

He stared into the empty room. Why had he suddenly said the words 'Don't leave me'? They had just popped into his head.

Then it struck him. It was the ghost who had grown to appreciate his friendly presence. She did not want to be left alone.

Johnny smiled at her, invisible, undetectable and somewhere just out of reach. He said: 'Don't worry. I'll be back in forty-five minutes.'

Joan Collins: A House With History

Introducing Joan Collins is about the most pointless task I will perform in this entire book. Surely everyone knows her? One of the bright stars of the British film industry stable in the hopeful days of the fifties, now she is just about the hottest Hollywood property going. Her Dynasty *role as Alexis (Carrington, Colby, Dexter or whoever she is married to in this week's show) may or may not be true to life, but she commands huge sums for her portrayal of steamy, scheming and powerful women.*

Verifying any story about Joan Collins is an arduous task, but I believe that my sources indicated this one to be true enough. It concerns the luxurious mansion in Bel Air that she purchased in 1985, from the proceeds of all her glittering successes.

If anywhere least qualifies for the term 'suburb', it is the sprawling tree-lined avenues of Bel Air, part of the huge star-studded megalopolis that is the Greater Los Angeles area. It shimmers in the heat and smog like a giant screen set and attracts visitors who ride around in tour buses, hoping (quite forlornly) to catch a glimpse of Charlton Heston or someone like him hanging out the washing. Yet, technically, a suburb is exactly what Bel Air, like

Beverly Hills and even Hollywood itself, really is. The actors commute from there to their mundane little jobs creating magic for cinema and TV audiences.

Joan is reputed to have paid over $3 million for her new abode. It naturally had a swimming-pool, plus eight bedrooms, so it had some things going for it.

It also had a minor problem – a curse.

At least, that is what her prospective neighbours advised, warning 'Joanie', as she is affectionately known, not to touch it with a jewel-encrusted barge-pole. That, of course, was about as useful as telling Hitler not to invade Poland. It only enhanced the intrigue and value of the property in her eyes.

But was there any substance for this peculiar suggestion? In a way, there was. It had claimed the lives of the stars Laurence Harvey (in 1973) and Totie Fields (in 1978). But then, this particular kind of house is noted for its short-term occupancy, and being a movie actor is not the most stable of occupations, nor the most respected by insurance-raters, so, perhaps, this was just sheer bad luck.

But then, I had heard that Totie was rather psychic herself. For instance, the singer/comedienne had an ongoing ESP rapport with her older sister, Ray. Once Totie had gone into a store, seen a suit that would be perfect for Ray, ordered it and told the shopkeeper that her sister would collect it later. But Totie was called away unexpectedly and never got a chance to pass on the good news. Then Ray went to the same store, saw a suit she thought would be perfect and ordered it – only to find that it was already reserved for her!

Whether Joan Collins knew of this, or indeed whether it has the slightest connection with Totie Field's tragic death or the so-called jinx now resident in the house, is quite another matter.

Yet the death of David Janssen in 1983 was not. Briefly, the star of the TV series *The Fugitive* suffered a nightmare in which he saw a coffin being carried out. Terrified, in the dream David asked who was in it and was told the rather disturbing news that it was some actor chappie called Janssen. He had a medical check-up but it was too late. Forty-eight hours after the dream, David had a massive heart attack and died. His coffin was carried out – from the house now on Joan Collins' shopping-list.

Despite the house's ill-fated pedigree, Joan handed over the dollars and took possession. Yet the sad saga of the jinxed mansion dragged on. She and Peter Holm quickly went through a much-touted public divorce, and as part of the settlement she lost this modest Bel Air dwelling to her former husband.

Somehow, I wonder who was the unlucky one!

Curses and jinxes are a difficult topic to evaluate. In my book Beyond Explanation? *I referred to how one was said to have struck the set of the British TV soap* Coronation Street, *when actor after actor began to die or suffer misfortune.*

I was heavily criticized for taking this seriously (not least by some of the cast of the Granada TV show, who were none too keen on living with a supernatural nemesis). But whether or not I was talking nonsense (as I fully admit I might well have been!), it must be remembered that curses are the product of belief in their powers. If a series of events occurs and you pin them on a jinx, the jinx springs to life, because it worms its way into the subconscious mind of some folk, causing all sorts of things to happen. People trip when they shouldn't, and worry about unseen forces.

Perhaps it is best not to take chances.

Commercial Break: Scriptwriters' Conference

With any TV show on a commercial network, there comes a time for a break. Normally that means adverts for cat food or soap powders (where the term 'soap opera' originated, of course). This also tends to be the signal to get up and make a cup of tea.

I promise that this break will be a little different. Before Episode Two in our series of mystery stories, let's make a slight diversion into the little-known world of a scriptwriters' conference. The idea is to look at some of the ways in which the paranormal has been slotted into modern TV series.

I am reminded of a line in the popular American show *Cheers*, set in a Boston bar. Woody, the farm boy now serving drinks in the big city, is asked if he believes in premonitions. 'No,' he reports, after much careful thought, 'but I have a strange, overpowering feeling that one day I will.'

Not all attempts at placing strange phenomena into the storyline are as successful, although there have been some gems.

Who can forget the long-running series *Soap*, the title itself showing the delightful intention to self-parody. Just about anything you could imagine (and a few things you could not) were crammed into the weekly episodes to demonstrate, with the subtlety of a turbo-charged steamroller, that scriptwriting in soaps *is* exactly like that.

A particularly enlightening sequence involved one of the principal characters, Bert, being abducted by a UFO and examined by its alien occupants. In order to ensure that no one sees the truth, an alien replacement for Bert is sent back to Earth, where he has attributes that Bert's wife finds rather appealing. The consequence is that a child is born, which, of course, may not be exactly one hundred per cent earthling and not especially nice to know.

On the one hand this is pure farce, but it is fascinating to see how close its elements (based in part on movies such as *The Exorcist* and *Close Encounters of the Third Kind*) were to reality. Actual cases of just this sort have since been claimed.

In 1987, several years after the cancellation of *Soap*, artist Budd Hopkins put together a book in which he related what he believes to be genuine stories of women abducted from Earth, impregnated by aliens and then having dreams of giving birth to inhuman children. These are fortunately taken from them to be raised on other worlds.[7]

This is curiously identical to the plot of *Soap*. But why is life imitating art? And which came first? Still, you may think, this could only happen in America.

Well, no. I investigated one such case myself, involving a woman from Cornwall, and there is no question she believed her experience to be real. As far as we could tell, she had not seen *Soap*, but it is preferable to think that she must have, back in the distant past, and then simply forgotten about it. Yet, even if she had, what relationship is there between the bedroom visit by a human-looking entity and the subsequent termination of her pregnancy?

A more subtle approach was adopted by the genteel Scottish TV series *Take the High Road*, set in a fictional village and filmed around Loch Lomond, north of Glasgow. It is a very successful export and has the sort of 'olde worlde' charm that is peculiar to British soaps.

In 1986 the idea of 'second sight', as ESP is still called in rural areas, was slotted into the storyline. One of the characters, a crofter named Inverdarroch, was persuaded by fellow farmers that he possessed the gift. In this way they aimed to get on his good side. They would claim that he entered a trance and gave out messages, explaining the whereabouts of missing sheep, for example. He could remember none of this when he 'returned', which was hardly surprising, as he had never been anywhere or said anything at all. Meanwhile, the others had put the sheep where Inverdarroch's ESP had predicted, and this reinforced his belief in his own special powers.

The ruse worked only because of people's ability to view the paranormal on a variety of levels. On the one hand we can treat it as amusing and accept that someone could be made a fool of, but that no real harm is done. On the other we can easily comprehend why the man, born and raised in a community where the supernatural is accepted as a way of life, would be fooled by relatively little evidence.

Take the High Road reflects certain truths about how and why people respond to the paranormal; other programmes have recognized the same fact. *Coronation Street*, Britain's longest-running TV soap, now heading towards its thirtieth year, has in its time introduced both ghosts and UFOs.

The *Coronation Street* ghost was never explained away and became accepted as a true encounter. It came about when the spectre of one of the regulars at the Rover's Return pub (Martha Longhurst) was seen sitting where she had always sat. A fine play on the tradition of haunted English public houses (of which there are many) and affording much scope for one-liners are about licensed premises that serve spirits.

The UFO invasion of Weatherfield, the fictional Salford district where the show is set, involved Curly, one of the characters who was at the time a dustbin man. Being a brainy type, he was scripted to be interested in astronomy and observed a strange phenomenon through his telescope.

In fact, the episode was handled quite accurately. Not only did Curly innocently report the experience and find that suddenly his simple account of witnessing something he could not identify had become glaring press headlines, such as 'Binman Boffin Spots UFO', but along came the debunkers and the detractors – just as in real life – who explained what he had seen as just about anything they could. As usual, the explanations were often more bizarre than accepting that something odd was seen in the first place.

This incorporation of story elements is only to be

expected. Interest in the paranormal is a part of modern society, and so it should be reflected in scripts. The trend is even culturally dependent. For instance, *Dynasty* has seen Blake Carrington habitually turn to psychics whenever all normal methods of problem-solving have failed. (Note also the real-life experiences of his screen wife, Linda Evans. See p.72.)

Blake (played by John Forsythe) employed them to try to trace his son Stephen, when he disappeared (and returned as a new actor with an entirely new face and voice). Such a tendency to use 'psychic detectives' is indeed more commonplace in the USA. It is only a matter of time before a psychic agency opens up in some city over there.

This is not to say that British police forces shun the help of mediums. I have looked into several bona fide cases where this has occurred.[8] But, in general, Americans are more willing to admit the adoption of unusual, not to say bizarre, methods. Most British detectives who have deserted their snouts for crystal balls have (I think, wisely) kept rather quiet about it.

Only very occasionally does a truly intelligent method of using ESP occur to soap scriptwriters. In the long-running private eye series where Tom Selleck plays Hawaiian-based *Magnum*, he frequently alludes to using intuition in solving cases (he calls it his 'little voice'). A number of the episodes have dealt with the paranormal in a sober manner.

Take, for instance, the 1985 show entitled 'Rapture' where Magnum sees a young boy whilst swimming under water. He becomes obsessed with the figure (who is not there) and starts to have dreams. His friends assume the private investigator has in fact suffered the effects of 'rapture of the deep', with hallucinations triggered by loss of oxygen to the brain. But he cannot believe it and eventually tracks the boy to source. The youngster died years before but his killer was never caught. By returning to the spot where the ghost had been seen, Magnum finds the vital clue and catches the man responsible.

Most series would have built in some cop-out. (The boy had never really died, for instance, or there was some other normal way in which the detective could have secured the information.) But *Magnum* is too sophisticated for that and, even though it means leaving question-marks about the plot dangling off the edge of a cliff, this is how it prefers to go.

Real life is the same. Especially when we are talking about the paranormal.

Sometimes the mystery is not so much fiction written into the plot but almost a hybrid between fact and fiction. I will show what I mean with a few examples.

In *Emmerdale Farm* Diana Davies plays estate secretary Mrs Bates. She was involved in what she called *déjà vu* when she read the ongoing script planned for her character.

Déjà vu is a sense of having seen something before. It is a feeling most of us get from time to time. What happened here was that Mrs Bates was to find her estranged husband returning, having previously run off with a younger woman without seeking divorce. Now he wants one, because his girlfriend has become pregnant.

What amazed Diana was that exactly this had happened to her in reality.

Of course, given the complexities of most soap operas, such a coincidence must crop up from time to time, just as it did in the award-winning series about women detectives in Manhattan *Cagney and Lacey*: in 1987 drama was injected into the storyline when Christine Cagney (played by Sharon Gless) suddenly lost her father; in real life, as she was recording that episode, the same tragedy struck.

The scripts took her on from this pressure into a battle with alcoholism. Superb performances saw Christine almost lose her job as she fought against the demon drink. In April 1988, shortly after filming these episodes, it was revealed that Sharon had secretly fought an almost identical battle and pulled through, just like her character in the series.

Again we can probably accept coincidence. But where does this end and something else begin?

The BBC have a soap often nicknamed *Dallas on Sea* but in truth entitled *Howard's Way*. This saga of a Hampshire boat-building firm has more twists and turns than a well-used capstan, and yet in real life many of the fictional dramas have come true.

Tony Castro, the man who designed the boat *Barracuda* for the TV series, was commissioned in 1988 to design a revolutionary new type of vehicle for the transatlantic race. This ran into legal problems when another competitor, New Zealand, argued that it was too revolutionary for their liking. Meanwhile, as this was still going on, in May 1988, the *Barracuda* foundered, creating new difficulties for the makers of the series.

Just a normal year in the life of boat-manufacturers perhaps. Yet many of these events had been fictionalized in one way or another in the *Howard's Way* series transmitted the year before they really happened.

That fact and fiction interlock in a peculiar kind of fashion is shown even more remarkably by the British soap *Crossroads*.

This story of a West Midlands motel will best be known as the first long-running series to succumb in modern times, closing its doors for good in 1988 after twenty years on air. But it ended in a puzzling manner.

Final scenes were shot in late 1987, with new storylines being necessarily stifled at birth. One that was beginning to go somewhere involved a young girl, Beverley, who had observed a UFO just before a group of paranormal researchers descended on the motel.

As the series acted out its death-throes, the ITV network decided to cut the transmission of pre-filmed episodes from three a week to two. This threw the timing of the show well off. The ones concerning the UFO (recorded in November) went out the following March, although the script clearly indicated that they had been related to Valentine's Day. This was because on basis of three episodes a week, they should have gone out in February.

Something weird resulted from this. The script again acted itself out in real life, without anyone's noticing. Between 15 and 18 February 1988 there was a sudden spate of UFO sightings. Dozens were recorded and many involved expert witnesses such as police officers. They centred on one part of the country, the West Midlands – in fact, *exactly* the same part of the West Midlands where the fictional motel was supposed to be having its UFO sighting that very week!

The *Crossroads* episodes had not been transmitted, so they did not *cause* the reports. Perhaps you suspect a plot afoot. The soap writers, in a final, desperate struggle for survival, went out and whipped up some real sightings to link with their storyline? But that makes no sense. The show had long been cancelled by February and the set broken up. Also, many of the cases were investigated and were undoubtedly genuine.

What is more, if there was a plot, I must have been part of it. I had written an article about waves of UFO sightings and media interest. This had been scheduled for publication in the respected British newspaper *The Guardian* well before these mid-February events, but it appeared right in the middle of the *Crossroads* wave, on 17 February.

Even more astonishing, I had been consulting since December on a TV debate about UFOs which was to go out live. We made this on 18 February, but it had been scheduled well prior to the sightings taking place. This programme was transmitted nationally by Central TV, the company that had been responsible for *Crossroads*.

It is sometimes tempting to think that there is little difference between real life and TV drama. I recall one week in October 1982 when I wrote a short story (later published as 'Don't Step in the Dark') concerning strange events in the Rossendale Valley of Lancashire, where I was born and raised. The story featured a bright red trials motorbike. That same week, the police soap *Juliet Bravo* screened an episode with exactly the same image. Just a coincidence? Maybe, but *Juliet Bravo* is filmed in the quiet Rossendale Valley and, lo and behold, that episode had a scene with a car parked right outside the house in which I first lived!

To end this review, here is how *Dynasty* handled their recent brush with the supernatural.

It began in late 1985, when a book by Peter Warrington and myself appeared in the USA. It was based on an article we had written for *New Scientist* magazine.[9] The book included a report on stories of people allegedly taken inside UFOs to be given strange examinations. All of a sudden, the idea that people could be kidnapped by aliens was major news.

At this point, *The Colbys*, which had started as a spin-off from *Dynasty*, was in trouble. It desperately needed to recapture audiences to compete in the big budget stakes. Soaps have an ongoing war with one another to come up with the most breathtaking last episode before an enforced summer recess. The thinking is that, if this is exciting enough, it is sure to bring viewers (and advertisers) scurrying back when the soap resumes in the autumn. Working on this principle, *Dallas* has had J.R. shot twice in the final episode, believing that a 'who done it' and 'will he/won't he pull through' debate will guarantee a big audience after several weeks off the air. This was the philosophy of the scriptwriters of *The Colbys*, who attempted to come up with an end-of-season episode to top the lot. Alien abductions were a craze (in a round-about way, thanks to me!), so what better to adapt? They spent half a million dollars and arranged a few fancy effects so that Fallon Colby (an American played by British actress Emma Samms) could ride into the sky as the credits rolled.

Being in such a rush to film for a May screening, they incorporated elements from recently published stories. This meant that a very stereotyped presentation emerged, and the aliens were not three-foot-tall eggheads with large, staring eyes (as in reality) but far cheaper to reproduce (and more appealing) male hunks in bacofoil suits.

None of this rescued *The Colbys*, which was cancelled after that episode, but several characters, including Fallon, were transferred back to *Dynasty* (from whence they had come in the first place). Having spent so much on these out-of-this-world scenes they had to transfer the plot as well. This gave the perfect excuse to replay the abduction scene about a dozen times, thus saving money in the new series.

After a medical examination, Fallon was deposited back by the aliens. She wandered around starry-eyed for a bit and was ensnared by a lady writing a book about abduction cases, who was desperate to include this one, but then lost her husband in the process. Jeff, the husband, thought that, rather than seeing little green men (or big, macho silver ones, as it turned out), Fallon ought to be seeing a psychiatrist. In fact, she already had, but the psychiatrist was a UFO freak and told her not to worry. Thousands of people got kidnapped every year by aliens from outer space, he said, and didn't she have any more unusual problems to bother him with? Meanwhile our heroine was starting to remember the nasty things that had happened on board the UFO – basically that these beings smelt of cinnamon and had leathery skin (a novel aspect of recent *actual* cases).

If by now you are becoming totally bemused by what is real and what is part of *Dynasty*, I can only say that so am I!

As all this hokum was being filmed and transmitted, I really *was* writing a book about women who had actually been abducted. Most of the things that were cooked up by the screenwriters had cropped up in the real cases I had found. This included marriages breaking up and (no doubt some of my witnesses might argue) the unscrupulous use of stories by a lady writing a book about abduction cases.

However, none of this beats what was to take place on the night of 12/13 February 1988 (remember the *Crossroads* UFO flap that same week?). In this episode of *Dynasty* it chanced (if any of this *was* chance!) to be the big moment of revelation, when Fallon finally discovers in a sudden flash of insight that her alien captors smelt like a spice rack and looked as if they had been out in the Californian sun too long.

One woman in Clayton-le-Moors, Lancashire, saw that episode. Just a few hours later, as she slept in her bed, she was whisked away by some very strange creatures. Yes, they had a complexion like wrinkled prunes and reeked ever so slightly of the light brown bark of a Sri Lankan tree. These spicy aliens gave a private repeat screening just for her, with the only major difference being that this was not on her TV set but in her house (and ultimately inside a real UFO).

You may well react just as I did, when woken with the

dawn still a twinkle in the eye of Saturday morning to learn this earth-shattering news. I concluded the woman had simply dreamt it all.

However, after investigation, the facts seem less than certain. The woman now claims that it really happened to her on 25 June 1987 and had only been triggered into her memory by watching TV the night before. *Dynasty* had coincidentally used the real-life story from her experience, not the other way around.

When you reach p.74, you will realize that this was twenty-four hours after the death of Jackie Gleason, who claimed to have met alien beings just like these – beings apparently still alive now and into major-league felonies, such as kidnapping and doing nasty things to unmentionable parts of women's bodies.

If by now you are convinced that the whole of life is indeed a soap script and that the dividing line between what you read in books, watch on TV and experience in real life is so elusive as to be unworthy of a search, you might read the rest of this book with new understanding.

On the other hand, you may prefer to regard all this as a sort of health-warning about the dangers of watching too many American soaps.

Episode Two: Tales of the Unexpected

Leslie Crowther: The Price is Fright

I remember Leslie when as a child I used to watch the famous BBC programme where people always seemed to be winning cabbages. I took Crackerjack *to be a subtle way of indoctrinating youngsters into eating greens, but there was evidently more to it than that. Leslie went on to become a top comedian and then relaunch his career in a big way by hosting* The Price is Right, *a long-running American game show, now on export (like hamburgers and Donald Duck and with passing similarity to both). The basic idea appears to be that you cram into a studio a few hundred people, who seem to have escaped from somewhere else, and get them to scream, shout, jump up and down and try to win an electric toothbrush. But Leslie steers this hugely popular mayhem into at least some semblance of respectability.*

Legends abound within show business, and most British theatres are blessed with a liberal sprinkling of ghosts. Of all spectre stories, the one in which Leslie Crowther plays a part is certainly the most unusual.

The pretty West Country city of Bath, with its monumental Georgian crescents, is the place where this affair is centred. The delightful streets that attract tourists by the coach load also boast the Theatre Royal, long-time home of much thespian activity.

Pantomime is a very British tradition around Christmas time. It involves a small number of fairy tales which are acted out, as if on a rota, across the country, with famous actors starring in almost ritual comedy performances and coveting the lead parts at the best locations. The 1938 pantomime at Bath was *Cinderella*, hosted by the Maddox brothers. Part of the scenery involved a tortoise-shell butterfly, and coincidentally during the opening-night performance the rare sight of a real creature was seen on stage. It was dead. Shortly afterwards Reg Maddox collapsed with a heart attack and died. So was born the legend.

Some years ago Leslie Crowther was taking part in the Bath pantomime – Aladdin, as it was that year. On the opening night a butterfly literally fluttered by onto the stage and landed right on top of the entertainer. It was attracted by the spotlight and flew around him for a few moments before resting on his jacket. He was stunned into silence.

The audience saw it, of course, but most of them did not know that it is claimed that, should a live butterfly appear on the opening night, it guarantees good luck and success for the production, whereas the appearance of a dead one heralds doom and gloom. They watched in astonishment as Leslie carefully picked it up and handed it, ever so gently, to a stagehand. Knowing the legend as he did, there was no way in which he was going to let the creature come to any grief.

Butterflies (or earthly ones, that is!) are exceptionally rare in late December, when Leslie's pantomime opened, yet the legend lived up to its reputation, and *Aladdin* went on to break box-office records. In researching this, I was given a great deal of help by Jane Wastie, from the administrators' office at the theatre.

Jane Wastie confirmed the Leslie Crowther story and that of the ill-luck brought by the dead butterfly in 1938. 'It has grown into a very strong legend,' she told me. 'We take it seriously, and so do the actors.' Indeed, the original 1938 set is still in the building. 'No one wanted to take responsibility for moving it,' she explained.

When I spoke with her Leslie Crowther was booked for his first return visit since the *Aladdin* show. He was to star in panto for the 1988-9 season, in *Robinson Crusoe*. Jane Wastie confessed: 'We are rather hoping another butterfly will turn up this time round.'

Patrick Duffy: Coping with Adversity

Along with Dynasty, Dallas *is the most successful of all the US* soap operas. It has been exported from America to most developed countries and run upon a vast budget for ten years. With its infamous character J.R., played by Larry Hagman, it has smashed TV records.

The other original Ewing brother was Bobby, the mirror image of his nasty fraternal sidekick. Patrick Duffy (who prior to this played a human fish in the series **The Man from Atlantis**) has portrayed Bobby throughout, with the exception of one series where he quit (vowing never to return under any circumstances). Thanks to this, he was killed off in spectacular fashion, and a whole year of shows followed with Bobby clearly dead. Then came a circumstance not foreseen (basically more money to pep up flagging viewing figures), and it was deemed vital that Bobby should return. Obviously his violent death in the previous series provided a slight obstacle to that requirement, but not to the intrepid **Dallas** scriptwriters. They formulated one of the most infamous get-outs in TV history. All the events in the previous twelve months' episodes (the ones following Bobby Ewing's death) were written off as never having happened. Instead they were just a dream by screen wife Pam (Victoria Principal).

However, this was quite an odd dream, because a new character had been introduced into the action (or rather the action that never happened, Pam merely having dreamt that it had). This character was a man who turned up at the ranch and later claimed to be Jock Ewing, the oil barons' father who had (at least viewers **thought** he had!) died in a previous series. As the scriptwriters wanted this plot in the new (post-dream) episodes, they decided not to junk it along with all the other aspects of Pam's dream (notably Bobby Ewing's death). Of course, in order to do that, they had to overlook the fact that Pam must have dreamt about this character **before** he was actually introduced in the new (post-dream) series. So Pam's dream must also have foretold the future (as well as saving the money mogul's bacon).

To have provoked that kind of gamble with the credibility of the plot (and, if you are not familiar with **Dallas**, you are bound to be now asking 'what credibility?') does at least illustrate the importance of actor Patrick Duffy to the soap. And if you found yourself completely lost trying to figure out any of the above explanation, please don't blame me. I don't write the **Dallas** scripts!

Patrick Duffy believes in life after death. Indeed, he is

convinced that we all get re-born into a new human body after this life ends.

This view comes from Buddhism, which Patrick went on to embrace with considerable gusto, despite the Catholic upbringing of his father, Terry. Indeed, this seems to have contributed to a rift that developed in the family, after Patrick left the mountain town of Boulder, Montana, for the bright lights of Hollywood. Terry and Marie Duffy stayed behind managing the small bar they had owned in that community for many years.

However, the rift was fast healing and Patrick's parents had nearly taken up his suggestion that they retire to California, when tragedy struck. On 18 November 1986 a row broke out in the bar over Terry Duffy's failure to serve two customers whom he considered the worse for drink. Shots rang out, and both Patrick's parents died beneath a horrific onslaught of bullets fired at very close range.

But for his faith in life after death, and the concept that his parents were paying off some kind of debt from a previous existence by dying in this way, Patrick Duffy might not have got through the aftermath of that terrible event. But his acceptance of this extraordinary paranormal phenomenon was the solace that allowed him to continue work on the *Dallas* scripts.

We must wonder whether this background of acceptability of paranormal phenomena was in any way relevant to something that reputedly took place in and around the set of this Texas soap, for it is alleged that the filming has been 'haunted' by the ghost of actor Jim Davis.

Davis had played the original oil baron, Jock Ewing, until his real death saw the character being written out of the series as a mark of respect. The weird saga seems to have begun when a photographer was taking publicity stills at the windswept Texan ranch that plays host to the Ewings when a series is in the making. The smiling and apparently very happy form of the unmistakable actor was seen by the swimming-pool, evidently watching the plans for the latest action with considerable affection.

From here the rumour spread that Jock had returned, and everyone kept their eyes open for supernatural goings-on.

Patrick Duffy was one of those who attested to the fact that strange things had indeed taken place. Along with Linda Gray (whose on-off marriage to J.R. Ewing is another regular feature of the soap), he thought that there was evidence in the antics of the mysterious oil-painting of Jock that has had a place in the series from the very beginning.

Although this massive work has hung in several locations (now being housed in the downtown Dallas offices of the fictional oil company), it was for much of the time in the great South Fork ranch house where the Ewings are supposed to reside.

Jim Davis was extremely fussy about this picture. As on most TV programmes, things tend to get moved about with the constant toing and froing of the many technicians who need to rearrange the props in between takes, so it was not uncommon for the portrait to get knocked out of true and droop a little on its hook. Jim never liked that to happen, so he took every opportunity of putting it straight. Of course, after his death the picture still got knocked about, and there was no one there prepared to make these constant readjustments.

Not that this apparently stopped the portrait from moving – all by itself!

Perhaps it is hardly surprising that, in the climate of rumour and belief generated by the story of Jock's apparition, the culprit for these actions was easy to find. The suggestion that Jim Davis was still looking after the portrait from the spirit world took hold and became a nice idea that was hard to disturb. Not that the publicity department of *Dallas* would ever dream of disturbing such a wonderful tale.

On a much more significant level, there was the experience of Barbara Bel Geddes, the actress who plays Miss Ellie, Jock's screen wife.

Being the only senior members of the cast (before the arrival of Hollywood legend Howard Keel), Barbara and Jim often used to chat happily about their juniors. After his death, she missed him and then became seriously ill. Indeed, she was replaced in the show by another actress (Donna Reed) when her indisposition became too bad to allow her to continue working.

Just at this point, when she was struggling to film episodes and considering her future with the series, Barbara thought she saw Jim Davis reflected in a window she was facing on the set. Her immediate reaction was that someone had moved the portrait and that it was simply visible in the glass. But a quick glance back showed that this was not the case.

Then she thought she heard a voice in her mind, which sounded like Jim Davis'. He was telling her to stick with the programme, because 'the kids need you'. This was an endearing term he had often used in life, and the experience, whilst puzzling and inconclusive, certainly made its mark.

Whether she heeded this spectral advice or not, Barbara fought her way bravely through the illness and returned to her role in *Dallas*. She has continued to play the much-loved part of the matriarchal head of the Ewing clan, and it is not only the 'kids' in the cast who are grateful for that. Millions of viewers all around the world are delighted too.

As for the stories about Jock Ewing's ghost, these continue to circulate but, as with most 'hauntings', especially very friendly ones such as this, no one can now tell fact from fiction. Particularly not when the media get their hands on the information.

You may rather wisely feel inclined to treat this particular phantom with a degree of caution. It is just the sort of tale you might imagine a soap opera's conjuring up to help promote itself. I found evidence for that in a number of other instances, but none here – which is by no means the same as saying that none exists. You can check it out for yourself. The South Fork ranch outside Dallas really does exist and has been attracting tourists from all over the world since the soap became a hit.

I suppose the real test will come if the image of Jock's ghost or one of these supernatural happenings ever gets captured on screen during the filming. It will be fascinating to see how the scriptwriters respond to an opportunity like that!

Michael Elphick: Strange Goings-On in the Ladies' Loo

Michael is a highly versatile actor who has appeared in stage, screen and TV roles for many years. He is currently appearing on BBC and ITV in widely differing roles. On ITV he is the star of Central's hit export Boon, *where he plays an urban cowboy riding around Birmingham on his motorbike to defend good against bureaucratic, villainous tyrants. And on the BBC he chuckles through episodes as an amateur taxidermist who is in love with his landlady in the immensely popular comedy series* Three Up, Two Down. *He is one actor who is instantly recognizable, with his soft Cockney accent fine-tuned by a smouldering, gritty realism.*

In *Boon*, the lead character, Ken, has left the fire service and helped his best mate buy and run a Midlands hotel. Most of the action and adventure have stemmed from that. In real life Michael Elphick has emulated this decision and has actually landed himself in a situation with even stranger overtones. He has come into confrontation with a ghost.

The real hotel is a very old building dating back approximately 600 years. Michael purchased it in 1987 with a business partner, just as in the TV series that made him an international star. Situated in lovely countryside midway between Birmingham and Stratford-upon-Avon, it is even in the same part of Britain as the fictional establishment in *Boon*.

The immediate area is actually noted for odd goings-on. In March 1980 a young subcontractor was driving nearby when a glowing shape darted across the narrow road ahead. Instantly he felt the steering-wheel begin to glow red hot and had to yank his hands away. Fortunately the experience was over in seconds, and he quickly regained control of the car.

Investigation of this incident suggested that, whatever the glow had been, it seems to have induced a current into the coils within the steering-wheel and so was presumably generating a rather considerable radiation or electro-magnetic field.

However, the traditions within Michael Elphick's nearby country hotel go back much further than that.

My investigations into these happenings at first reached a fairly reluctant staff. For this reason I have not named the hotel or its exact location, as not surprisingly, they were wary of the attention being accorded it and assumed I was a journalist who had picked up on the Michael Elphick connection in an effort to manufacture a sensational story. Indeed, this reluctance to sell the story to me was impressive, for I had the feeling that this was no publicity gimmick but a genuine apparition that was simply not talked about too openly.

One of the staff members told me in a guarded way that they knew of the claims regarding a female ghost in a certain part of the building, but she was reluctant to talk further without her employers' approval. Eventually I succeeded in reaching Mrs Vandrill, the woman who, along with her husband, co-owned the building with the celebrated actor.

She acknowledged the situation: 'Something has been seen by people in the past, but not by anyone lately, so far as I believe. There has been a lot of talk about it in the village. Rumours and so forth. But these are just the sort of stories that grow up around any old building, I imagine.'

Naturally, I suspected that these accounts had been fostered by Michael Elphick's involvement and that some cynics might well suggest that the tales were conveniently good publicity for him and for the hotel. But the manageress was very honest and insistent: 'No. This is not a publicity stunt. The stories exist. They existed before Michael came here and before we came here. I certainly haven't seen anything myself, I should add.'

I tried to probe a little deeper into the affair to discover exactly what is supposedly involved.

From staff members I learnt that one specific part of the establishment is regularly linked with the stories. This was, in fact, a section of the original building before modern extensions and alterations. The area concerned is now used for the ladies' conveniences, and so the staff must by necessity visit the spot quite frequently.

I could find no one who admitted to having seen anything, although some reluctance to tempt providence was in evidence. One young woman told me: 'About twenty years ago the figure of a woman in white was seen there. She was gliding along the landing. I gather it is not a very precise outline, just a vague, shadowy form, but it is always the same one that is seen and always in that one position.'

Mrs Vandrill confirmed this for me: 'Yes, I would say it is the spot on the landing that is said to be haunted rather than the whole building. And from my experience it is not so much something that is seen as something felt. A kind of cold sensation. It's almost as if the temperature drops right down as you pass by.'

I learnt of the experience related by the mother of a current staff member, who was herself working there some years ago. She felt this chill on the landing and was convinced that it originated from the white lady phantom.

'It was scary at the time. But that seems to be the only thing experienced in recent years, and nobody is particularly bothered by it now.'

'We don't have any problem getting the staff to visit the toilet,' the manageress calmly pointed out.

So far as I can ascertain, Michael Elphick has not experienced anything himself. 'He has been here and he knows all about the stories. But he is very happy. He finds it a very cheerful place. In any case, what is there to be disturbed about? The apparition is harmless enough. If there *is* something there, it doesn't bother us.'

Overall, I was convinced that a genuine ghost tradition does exist at this hotel. Also there was a refreshing absence of evidence that it was being hyped up as a publicity stunt. I asked the owners if they would approve a scientific investigation by researchers. I was told: 'I don't know if you would find anything. In any case, I think it's best to leave the place as it is. To take no chances and not disturb the peace.'

Linda Evans: In Search of Power

Linda Evans is a member of the cast of Dynasty *who has been with the series from the start. In soaps (where characters change actors at the same rate as some actors switch toupés), that is quite an achievement. Born in Hartford, Connecticut, she has also appeared in movies and mini-series but is best known for her part as Blake Carrington's wife. You will note that another ongoing competition in the world of soaps is to see who can invent the most unlikely name for a character.* Dynasty *features such everyday names as Bliss, Sable and Fallon, but how many secretaries (which is what Linda Evans' role was in the beginning) start out called Krystle? You will see in a moment why that in itself is an interesting little synchronicity.*

Shirley MacLaine, who also features in this story, is a very successful movie star but not especially known as a soap actress. However, there are those who have read her long series of books,[10] which recount her endless adventures in the psychic world, who believe that her entire existence is one long soap opera. Whilst her most bizarre adventures have indeed been turned into the TV series Out On A Limb, *the one problem with this 'life's a soap' hypothesis is that no scriptwriter could have conjured up some of the things which Shirley claims have really happened to her.*

If, according to legend, the streets of London are paved with gold, those of Los Angeles are paved with psychics. Everywhere you go in this sprawling city, particularly in its Hollywood area, there are gurus who have set up shop as if they were the owners of just another local deli. They vie with each other for the services of their rich clientele, using the latest techniques that are available.

Once upon a time, pyramids were all the rage. Based on what they did for the Egyptians, there was a theory that they could preserve razor blades, sharpen pencils and double your money overnight. Philip Michael Thomas, star of *Miami Vice*, is said to have slept with a six-foot one, and I suppose you could argue that it did him no harm.

But now things have changed, and the new fad is

crystals. Not any old crystal, you should understand. They have to be quartz.

Apparently, or this is what Shirley MacLaine reckons anyhow, they vibrate with energy, and the trick is to get that vibration to resonate with the natural frequency emanating from your own psyche. If you can manage this, good health, good looks, indeed just about anything, will result.

I suspect there are a few cynics reading this who consider the idea preposterous. Well, crystal therapists are becoming ever bolder, and quite a few stars seem eager to deplete their bank accounts to spend their money on the new system. Cybill Shepherd, from the hit series *Moonlighting*, is a regular customer, and her mother seems to believe that wearing quartz will enable her daughter to have even greater success.

It would be nice if crystals proved the answer to the prayers of Linda Evans (alias Krystle Carrington), but, so far, we do not know if this is the case. Certainly she has been asking for assistance from Shirley MacLaine, who has now begun to lecture and offer advice as the most celebrated of all the Hollywood psychics, a kind of paranormal agony aunt.

Linda's problem is that she is in her mid forties and time is fast running out to achieve motherhood, her greatest desire. Understandably she has turned to unorthodox methods of trying to resolve these difficulties. 'Doctor' Shirley has, in fact, prescribed a few colours.

Colour therapy may sound just as daft as crystals, but evidently it has its admirers. The idea is that each colour helps the mind tune into those magic frequencies and alter the state of consciousness. Once at the right level, it becomes possible for our psychic potential to be unleashed and to control our own body states.

At least, that is the theory.

Linda has a colour of orange that reflects sexuality, and this is naturally the key to her success in being able to conceive. What she must do is meditate on this hue and then lead herself into that state where she can bring about the bodily changes that are necessary.

Doubtless, if this works, it will all become crystal clear,

but in the meantime it is certainly a different way of trying for a baby.

You might think that I am rather sceptical of all of this. In fact, there are some grounds for supposing that quartz crystals might work in the way suggested.

For example, UFO researchers have long puzzled over why there are certain parts of the world that attract more sightings than others. They call them 'window areas'. It is now considered likely that these zones are dependent upon the type of rock that exists there. The presence of geological fault lines to produce stress is also vital. The rocks in major window areas, such as the Pennine Hills in northern England and the Brown Mountains of Missouri, have a high incidence of – you guessed it – quartz crystals!

This is not pie-in-the-sky theory either. It has been tested in the laboratories of the US Bureau of Mines in Boulder, Colorado, and replicated in Britain by scientists, such as geologist Dr Paul McCartney. So persuasive have their results been (even film showing glowing mini-UFOs stimulated by subjecting lumps of the offending rock to enormous pressure) that they have been favourably reported in sources such as New Scientist.[11]

One idea is that the crystal gives out the sort of electrical signal when squeezed that powers a quartz battery. This provokes a chemical reaction in the atmosphere directly above, creating the dazzling UFOs.

Jackie Gleason: A Date With Destiny

It is difficult for anyone who is not an American to understand the importance of Jackie Gleason. In that country he was a phenomenon; a comedy actor who transcended such a description and whose TV series The Honeymooners *gets as many reruns as* Star Trek. *His death in 1987 was a national disaster. I chanced to be in the USA when it occurred and knew little about the man. A dozen news flashes, front-page stories in major newspapers and cancelled schedules later, I was much wiser. Virtually every station inserted specials about the performer, dropping almost anything to accommodate them. I wonder if as much care would go into the televised obituary of many leading politicians. In every sense, Jackie Gleason was a big man.*

One night in 1973 Jackie Gleason returned home and sat down in a chair ashen-faced. He told his second wife, Beverley, that he had just seen the dead bodies of some alien beings.

Hearing that from a comedian, most of us would have looked hard to find the joke. Seeing the expression of shock on his face, Beverley Gleason sought only to understand this incredible admission.

According to her version, Jackie had earlier that day been invited onto Homestead Air Force Base in Florida by his close friend Richard Nixon, then President. It was here that the earth-shattering news was revealed and the final definitive proof displayed in front of his disbelieving eyes.

As Steven Spielberg would put it – indeed, *did* put it five years later – 'We are not alone.' After seeing what Jackie Gleason saw, no other conclusion was possible.

The aliens, according to Gleason, were just two or three feet tall, with large, domed heads. They had been retrieved from a UFO that had crashed over twenty years before.

Of course, this is a fantastic story. It was made even more fantastic by Jackie Gleason's reluctance to confirm it. Whilst he had no apparent qualms about his wife's making it public (and he himself had surely recognized the security implications but had still told her), he later refused all attempts to coerce him into elaborating.

Larry Bryant, a clerical officer with the government in Washington, DC, has for many years pursued the truth about the so-called 'UFO cover-up' and has used the nation's Freedom of Information Act to appeal for and obtain once-secret files on the subject.

I met him on a recent trip to the States, and he struck me as a very dedicated and rational man. He had certainly achieved some successes and, with others, showed me hundreds of official files that had been released. These included some that referred to a UFO that crashed in the New Mexico desert in 1947, from which were 'retrieved' dead aliens precisely like those described by Jackie

Gleason. There was even an affidavit signed by a doctor who said he had performed a secret autopsy on one of these entities.

Gleason was known to be interested in the paranormal. He was even a subscriber to the oldest regular publication in the field, *Fate* magazine. So he certainly would be aware of these tales of crashed UFOs. Also 1973 happened to be the height of interest in UFOs in the USA, when thousands of reports were made, generating much excitement.

But would Jackie Gleason joke about something like this, even to his wife? One thing was known. He *was* indeed a good friend of Nixon. That much at least made sense. But was it enough?

Larry Bryant tried to find the truth. However, Gleason would not respond. When he was asked face to face by a UFO sympathizer in the film industry, he still declined to answer. That is suggestive but was not proof.

So Bryant took to using other channels. He endeavoured to place an advertisement in the newspaper on Homestead Air Base. They refused him permission to do so. Meanwhile he appealed for documentation of the visit by either Gleason or President Nixon during 1973 but was told there were no such files. Eventually, in April 1987, Bryant won a court case giving him the right to pay for an advertisement in the base paper. As I write, he has reported no success with it.

When Jackie Gleason died, he took with him the answer to this strange mystery, and we may never know whether he did or did not see those aliens.

Most people will find it very difficult to believe the word of one of the world's greatest comedians when he says he saw the ultimate proof of alien existence. Yet there is no question that a good deal of evidence is on his side, and a great many people other than Gleason would have to be lying if none of this is true. For example, there are now hundreds of folk all over the world who say they have met alien entities that look exactly like the ones that were reputedly on that Florida air base.[12]

However, this does not disguise the fact that there are problems. How could such a momentous event be kept secret for what is said to be forty years? More importantly, why would it be kept secret? There are hints and clues in the released documents and reactions of world governments, but it is still hard to conceive such a major affair's being so effectively hidden for so very long. Think of Watergate and the Iran arms affair! Particularly if presidents were able to invite personal friends to see the aliens for themselves. That hardly suggests strict security.[13]

On 24 June 1987 I arrived in a sticky and sweltering New York City for a number of reasons. That day was the fortieth anniversary of a sighting in Washington state, when a pilot reported seeing objects over the Cascade Mountains. These objects had skipped through the air 'like saucers over water', and from this account the media invented the term 'flying saucer'. A mystery was born.

I had a book out celebrating those four decades and was also taking part in a panel discussion on government secrecy at a conference to be held at the American University in Washington, DC. It was there that I saw some amazing documents, then newly released, which had been sent anonymously on a roll of film to Jaime Shandera, a Los Angeles TV producer. These purported to be a briefing document to the US president explaining all about the crash of a UFO in 1947 and the capture of dead alien bodies. The aliens were exactly like those reported fourteen years earlier by Jackie Gleason.

What is the status of these astonishing files? There is still much controversy. Many are convinced they are authentic. Others say this is all a giant hoax. But why would Jackie Gleason be involved in a conspiracy?

A few months before my visit to the USA, I was approached by a military source in Britain, offering extensive documents which included autopsy details of dead aliens. I think you can guess the description of those beings. After making extensive enquiries, I had reason to conclude that the person offering the files was probably sincere but that someone else was using him to try to spread disinformation.

Exactly why there should be a plot to create the impression that the US government has successfully hidden the bodies of dead aliens for all these years is an even more fascinating question.

It is possible that Jackie Gleason might have known the answer, but with an eerie sort of irony he died on that very day I arrived in the USA, 24 June 1987, the exact day, in fact, on which the UFO phenomenon celebrated its fortieth birthday.

Perhaps someone was trying to tell us something!

Don Henderson: Visions of Death

Viewers in Britain will know Don for his roles in many TV series, including long-running dramas such as The Onedin Line *and* Poldark. *His gravelly voice has more recently made him a star as the ex-detective turned private eye George Bulman, who has been one of the few characters to survive through three differently named series that have followed his career. In the USA his TV work is known, but he may be better remembered for his movie parts. In* Star Wars, *for example, he was a wicked general in Darth Vader's battlestar.*

Don Henderson has visions of the future and is horrified by them. He sees death and tragedy before they happen and has no way of controlling the experiences or preventing their taking place. He feels helpless in the face of such unwelcome power.

In 1985 he was filming the early run of programmes in the *Bulman* series. In the story, the former tough policeman has retired to run a clock-repair shop in London (although clever disguise and the strategic use of one red London bus and an *Evening Standard* news van obscure the fact that the shows are actually made in Manchester!).

One episode was called 'Sins of Omission', written by Murray Smith. The plot required Bulman's young Scottish sidekick, Lucy (alias Siobhan Redmond), to be kidnapped whilst taking on dangerous work for the secret services. However, she is rescued by Pushkin, a KGB agent who has appeared in a number of previous episodes (even in the earlier incarnation of the show, when it was called *Strangers*). To do so, the Russian, who has a kindly love/hate relationship with Bulman, goes out on a limb and has to flee Britain unsure of his fate when the Soviets find out about his exploits.

The final scene in the episode was, Don Henderson explains, filmed in the basement of an old city warehouse across the road from the Granada TV studios. The script called for a very emotional parting as Don bids farewell to his Russian friend, played (as usual) by veteran actor George Pravda. Virtually the last scene sees Don and George hug one another, and Don whisper, in Russian, 'Goodbye, old friend.' Great emotion is to be injected as the camera closes in and then pans out. After all, the two men are parting without knowing whether they will ever meet again.

The scene was filmed, and it was wonderful. The production crew were stunned by the authenticity of it all. But, later, very quietly, Don was to admit that something had haunted the make-believe of that dark and cold set. As he had looked into the face of George Pravda, he had felt a peculiar sensation welling up inside and knew that it was more than the part that was getting him down. A voice was tickling the inside of his mind, explaining that he really *was* losing a friend, as the screenplay said, and that George Pravda's fate, just like the character Pushkin's, was hanging in the balance.

Somehow he knew that they would never meet again, although he realized that future scripts would dictate the Soviet's return. The tears of farewell were real tears, all the more poignant because Don Henderson knew of his ESP and his many other visions of death.

The film was canned, and shortly afterward the series was transmitted. But it was minus one avid viewer. George Pravda had suffered a fatal heart attack which struck out of the blue. He died before *Bulman* made it onto the screen.

Shirley Stelfox, whom we shall meet in greater detail later on, is Don's wife and a television actress.

'Terribly weird things happen,' she explains. 'The sort of experience you just try to put down to coincidence. They are usually quite minor ones, things that form a part of everyday life. Don will say something about a particular person – maybe a politician, for example. The next day there is a story in the paper, and it is just what Don said about them.'

I asked her to give an example. She said that there were many to choose from: 'I remember that he came home one Wednesday night. Like most of his experiences, curiously enough, this one happened when he was travelling in his car. He just said to me on arrival, "Did you hear about Torville and Dean?" '

Shirley explained why this immediately surprised her: 'Don is not the least interested in ice-skating or sport. To be honest, I found the very fact that he even knew the names, Torville and Dean, quite amazing.'

Apparently, he had heard a story on the car radio as he drove back home. The announcer had stated that the couple had achieved 'complete marks' and, as he worded it, 'This is unprecedented in world skating.'

Don had not considered there to be anything odd about this. It was just an off-the-cuff mention of a radio news item. But Shirley was baffled. 'I told him, "I didn't think it was the final", even though there was a championship on at the time. However, I was intrigued and watched the TV. I had been correct. It was not the final. When the marks were given for Torville and Dean, they were very good – mostly 5.9s – but they were certainly not perfect. I told Don this. I said, "You were wrong. They didn't get all sixes." He looked at me, and you could see he was annoyed that I did not believe him. "It *was* on the radio and that IS what the man on there said," he insisted.'

Shirley continued with the story: 'Three days later, on the Saturday, it was the final. We watched it, and sure enough they did set this incredible world record by getting all sixes. What is more, the TV announcer used the exact same words when describing the feat that Don had said he heard on the radio bulletin when coming home in his car.'

When this kind of thing happens, it opens up turmoil in the household. Shirley explained to me: 'They are usually quite small things like that. But they happen so often. At least once a week. You know that it just cannot be put down to chance. Don waits for it to happen, then says, "Oh my God, there it goes again." '

Having premonitions on such a regular basis can prove a very difficult thing for people to live with. I have found this myself, from studies of my own dreams. I certainly have premonitions. I believe that many people share in this but barely remember when it happens. There seems to be a kind of automatic process that represses the memory.

Scientific studies of premonitions show that they relate most often to two types of event, the trivial minutiae of life and the big disasters.[14] It is no real surprise for a student of the paranormal to learn that Don Henderson's experiences also range across these same two areas.

The minor events are in his personal life. The others seem to have great emotional attachment and make their mark *because* they have a deep impact on him after they occur. In this way, they form a strange sort of vicious circle. We are left to wonder whether he has the premonition because the tragedy affects him or whether (as he believes) the events disturb him more because he has foreseen them. This is not a dilemma which would appear to have an easy resolution.

Again, these terrible scenes occur most often in the car. 'Once he was driving along and he suddenly got this flash picture in his mind. It came out of nowhere, as if the scene had been lit up by this giant flashbulb. In the frozen frame he could see a car that had overturned. Every detail of the accident was embedded in his mind. Then it was gone.'

As Shirley told me, 'This is awful for him. Nobody understands how badly it affects him. He does not like talking to people about it, because they treat it as a joke or as something supernatural. Yet to him it is something really quite awful.'

In the case of the overturned car, as in many less dramatic incidents, he seems to soak up the emotion of the accident. 'He has to pull over the car to the side of the road,' Shirley points out. 'He cannot carry on driving. He has to stop to recover. Then he drives on and the scene is acted out in reality before the journey is over.'

That is what happened in this particular example. It was just a few minutes after getting the flash image that he really drove past the site where the accident had happened.

It is easy to see why this sort of thing would bother someone. There are grounds for believing that creative and caring people suffer from ESP more than others, because they are able to soak up the emotions of the experience. Having done so, just as an actor would when immersing himself in a part, they can then take all the pain and suffering into themselves, and this makes premonition of a tragedy very difficult to come to terms with.

'Don asks what he can do,' she told me. 'But there does not seem any way he can stop the thing from happening. This makes it much harder to cope with.'

Ironically, Don has appeared in a TV drama with the remarkably appropriate title *The Captive Clairvoyant*.

It would seem that premonitions happen when emotional shock-waves from an event spread out like ripples when you drop a stone into a pond. As you cut across the pond, heading for the spot where the stone has fallen, you can detect the event before you get there as you intersect the ripples spreading out. Most people have a barrier that prevents this. Our conscious mind has erected barricades that block the information, so that it filters through only in rare and occasional circumstances, or else, perhaps, during sleep, when the drawbridge is raised up a little bit.

People such as Don Henderson, on the other hand, are used to opening themselves up to absorb other people's feelings in order to play a part. This means that sometimes the emotions of a real tragedy sneak through the barricades and produce a psychic experience.

These are by no means the only psychic experiences involving Don Henderson. Others are also part of the story of his wife, fellow actor Shirley Stelfox. Later in the book you will find an interview with her that brings this out into the open.

Gary Holton: Auf Wiedersehen, Gary

The tragic young life of Gary Holton ended in 1986, when he was only thirty-three and had just recently made it into the big time. After parts in movies such as Quadraphenia *and toying with music stardom (including chart success in Scandinavia), he had* been an enormous hit as the Cockney likely lad Wayne in the unexpectedly successful saga of a group of out-of-work bricklayers. Shortly after work began on the continuing series of Auf Wiedersehen, Pet *adventures, Holton died – it is believed from a drugs overdose. Miraculous editing retained his part in the storyline without the insensitivity of 'killing him off'.*

Debbie Linden, who also features in this tale, is becoming well known in the USA, where the old standard British series Are You Being Served? *has turned into a surprise hit. Debbie played the bimbo secretary of the geriatric boss for several years in that show.*

A beautiful actress and former page-three girl, Debbie Linden knew from personal experience the danger of drugs. She had also been a close friend of Gary Holton, having worked with him on a series of television commercials. When he died, she was naturally very upset, but she claims that within twenty-four hours she saw the figure of Holton materialize in her bedroom and heard the words 'Stay off drugs' in her mind.

Whilst Debbie was not taking drugs, she was aware of the risks of falling back into old habits and took the warning very seriously.

The ghost of the TV star was nothing like the traditional image of a spectre. 'He looked as large as life,' Debbie insisted and seemed to be both conscious and aware of the fact that he had died and that drugs had destroyed him prematurely. He performed in his typical manner of switching from the live-wire comedian to the serious professional in a matter of moments.

Allegedly this apparition returned to the bedroom on a number of occasions over the next couple of weeks, and the young actress was terrified by his presence, despite their affection in life. She was so upset that she eventually fled the building and consulted a medium, who explained that this sort of post-mortem warning by an apparition is not uncommon, if it believes there is an important purpose to fulfil.

Whatever the case, the ghostly message found its mark, and Debbie insists she is not going to take drugs under any circumstances.

Eddie Large: Someone Up There Likes Me

Of course, Eddie Large is not the real name of this gregarious performer. But it seems appropriate. His TV shows are too numerous to mention, but he has been spotted a few times in the stands at Maine Road football ground, where, he has been for many years a fanatical supporter of Manchester City. Indeed, he had a promising career as a footballer with the team until an injury ended his prospects. He went on to emulate the prowess of many of the current playing staff and became a comedian.

It had been an ordinary day training with the club. Riding his bike away from the mudbath that passed for a pitch in those days, Eddie got a wheel stuck in an old tramline and was dragged into the path of a bus. Whilst he suffered leg injuries, he escaped with his life.

This is by no means the only time Eddie has cheated death. Once he fell over a cliff in the Pennines and saved himself by grabbing hold of the only tree anywhere in sight, a miraculously instinctive reaction. Another time, he crashed his van through a wall over the moors and walked away unhurt, with the van perched like a see-saw on the lip of a huge and certainly fatal plunge – inevitable, had momentum carried him only inches further.

Not surprisingly, Eddie suspects that someone 'upstairs' might be watching after him. And it may be that his parents have something to do with this.

When they died, he called the famous medium Doris Stokes – like just about everyone else in the television world, it seems. Doris, a big fan of his, immediately invited Eddie round to her home. At once his parents came through, and she saw snatches of images in her mind, which she repeated as best she could.

Did his mother have auburn hair? She did. Why was there a child in spirit which his mother was looking after? Because Eddie had lost one.

He left, seemingly another satisfied customer of this amazing woman. At least they had one thing in common, which they could share jokes about – their considerable volume.

I will not elaborate on Doris Stokes. I never met her, so it would be unfair to comment. One must judge from the endless successes claimed in her books.[14] I have interviewed her namesake, equally successful and also a confidante to the stars, Doris Collins. Having done so, I remain to be convinced that the messages might not be coming from the mind of the sitter rather than from the dead personalities they believe themselves in touch with.

Susie Mathis: A Special Anniversary

Susie is best known in the north-west, where she has had her own successful radio series for some years. Originally with commercial networks, she has recently switched allegiance to the BBC, for whom she has also presented TV specials. Those who have not seen her on TV might remember her days in the swinging sixties as a pop star with the all-female chart group The Paper Dolls.

It was 29 May 1986 and the scene was a tiny room at the BBC studios in Manchester. I was calling the shots, controlling a supernatural experiment and attempting to prove life after death – all in one afternoon, washed down by endless plastic cups of infamous BBC coffee.

Fiddling with the microphone, I introduced Totty, a sweet lady from Lancashire who claimed, without a trace of pretension, that she was a medium. She was not rich or famous. She never charged money or appeared on chat shows. She simply believed that voices and pictures came into her mind and conveyed information about the people she was sitting with. Without further question, she had agreed to this live experiment (one world-famous medium had refused outright), being told only that she would have a session with a celebrity and that, good or bad, the results would be reported.

I introduced her to Susie Mathis, whose name she recognized. But there was no way that Totty could have come prepared or found out the subject of the experiment in advance. However, the old lady smiled and said, 'I knew it was going to be you. I suddenly heard your name when I was in bed a few days ago.'

Also in the room was a man whom I introduced as 'Alan'. Totty had no reason to assume he was anything other than a BBC technician or producer. In fact, he was Professor Alan Smithers, a university psychologist. I wanted him there to watch what happened, so that he could comment later.

We all sat nervously round a heavily stained, litter-strewn table in sound-proofed silence. We were cut off as completely as an isolation booth in a TV game show. Totty, brushing it all aside, talked in bubbling animation. 'Ooh!' she exclaimed, 'I'm getting a lot of turmoil. Oh dear! I was given to understand that you had moved and there was a terrific amount of turmoil involved. Will it never end? But it's got to – with a move.'

Susie gazed on, and each time she tried to respond, Totty cut in politely, reminding her to say nothing and adding that some mediums cheat by watching for reactions. 'You must have a poker face,' she said gently. 'Just hear me out and say nothing.'

The session continued. Information about an old woman in a long black dress standing with arms folded in a butch manner. A very direct grandfather. Sleeping-problems. It all just tumbled out. Then she said, repeating a message from some unseen person, 'When the offer comes for you to go south – tell her to go. She'll enjoy herself, but you're not going as a permanency.'

However, the bulk of the half-hour sitting took the theme of a child. Totty's eyes lit up as if she had just picked up the news: 'There's a little baby that's passed, and he's telling me how it can be that the little boy who hadn't the power of words can converse. It's the power of the mind, you see. Babies grow quickly in the next stage of life. I don't know why I'm saying this to you. But there must be a reason.'

Professor Smithers and I sat implacable and bemused. Susie maintained a discreet silence. Then Totty concluded: 'I must keep on this theme about infants. They reach a maturity that they would reach if they had been allowed to live in a physical body. A baby under a year can reach twenty-three or twenty-four in a very short space of time.'

There had been no candles flickering or Spiritualist claptrap. It had, I suppose, been a seance, but, in truth, to us all it had just been a normal conversation. Totty ended, turned to Susie (as did I) and said, 'Well?'

Susie Mathis was evaluating the messages. Most of it did fit, in a general way (a picture of a great-grandmother who had looked and stood as Totty had suggested, a grandfather who really was as she described).

What about the turmoil? 'That's one hundred per cent right,' the entertainer confirmed. It had resulted from her transfer to the BBC, which had brought some professional acrimony. 'I've just been through what I hope is the worst period of my life,' Susie acknowledged. But with scrupulous honesty she admitted that many big news stories had reported it. I had read it myself in several daily papers, and so the medium could easily have recalled this. Although Totty answered, when I put this to her, 'I get the *Mirror, Sun* and *Star* but only ever do the bingo', it was hardly prime evidence.

The trip south was much more interesting. Totty probably could not have known about this, but Susie was then about to go south, with the prospect of a major job on the BBC's Radio Two network. She did go for a trial period, and enjoyed it, but, as Totty had said, it was not to be a permanent move. That did come soon after, with a switch of house.

Yet there was something lurking in the session that staggered us all, because it was not known to any of us other than Susie. And Totty cannot have been familiar with this information.

The clearly astonished Susie Mathis began cautiously; 'When you said about the message from the baby under a year … Ah, I did lose a baby a year ago. That's unbelievable that you should say that.'

In fact, Susie had always wanted a child and had even consulted the famous test-tube baby pioneer Dr Patrick Steptoe. He had ruled out any chance that she would ever conceive. He was wrong. She became pregnant, only to lose the child before it was born. It was a terrible wrench.

Susie Mathis juggled calendars in her head and looked at us in confused amazement. The unborn baby – which Totty said had now grown to maturity and was talking to his mother from beyond death – had 'passed over' *exactly* one year before this session.

Totty had also offered information to Professor Smithers, but he insisted that none of it was correct. She had spoken of Scotland, writing books, being a researcher into the paranormal in a sceptical fashion, an invitation to go to the USA the following spring thanks to some 'backing'.

None of this may have meant anything to the psychologist, but it did to me. Almost everything fitted recent events in my life, except the US trip. But six months later I was invited over, with part of my expenses paid in return for a lecture at a university. I went in June, which, given British weather, better qualifies for the term 'spring' than 'summer'.

What about Susie Mathis? She was impressed but kept all that had emerged in admirable proportion. 'I have a very open mind about things like this,' she told me calmly.

Commercial Break:
Forward Planning

One of the perils of an actor's life is living from day to day never knowing what tomorrow might bring. This insecurity is so rife that it might help explain why so many of the breed seem happy to spend long spells, even lifetimes, playing the same character in a TV soap. Variety is usually important, but a long-running series represents the acting equivalent of a steady job.

Another by-product of this uncertainty is the affinity actors seem to have with psychics and mediums. Perhaps even more than most of us, they want to know whether that big break will arrive with the show on current offer or even if they will still have a job after the reviews come out.

Occasionally this can have amusing consequences.

In soap lore there is an annual ritual: making the decision as to whether an actor should be retained. Often this will depend upon whether the US networks decide to continue a show, and money factors always play a big part. For instance, in 1988 the Emmy award-winning series *St Elsewhere* was cancelled because the programme-makers did not want it any more. Its audience was growing, and its actors all wished to carry on, but in the world of soaps money talks.

The real big-budget epics, such as *Dynasty* and *Dallas*, which cost millions of dollars per series to shoot, have another difficulty. Their very success brings ever higher demands for massive salaries from their top performers. They are being paid more than most Hollywood film stars, but the theory goes that, if the public want to see them and the financiers are raking it in, so should the actors.

Balancing all this together requires decisions every

summer about whether a star can still be afforded. To curb over-zealous demands, they are often put into a perilous position by the scriptwriters of the final episode in each series. In this way the producers can easily kill them off if they have asked too much. This is supposed to leave the members of the cast feeling dispensable and to restrain the spiral of inflated rises each year.

With a series like *Cagney and Lacey*, it has most often been a question of whether the two principals, Tyne Daly and Sharon Gless, *want* to make more episodes. For the last few years a 'will they, won't they?' situation has developed. The show is very popular around the world, particularly amongst female viewers, who see it as a portrayal of the modern successful career-woman. However, there is always the urge for the actors to use this recognition to build towards other things and take on new challenges.

In the 1987 summer break the dilemma was at its height for Tyne and Sharon, who had already agreed that, if either one wanted to go, that would be the end of it. The indecision kept everyone on their toes and finally, partly in jest, the production team brought in a psychic to sit with the two stars.

She read their palms and, of course, passed on the news that they should (would?) be staying with a series that has won more awards than any other in recent times. One wonders how the poor palmist could possibly have given any other advice, even had she wanted to. The mood was such that she would probably have been lynched by the crew, who all felt the show must go on.

After the readings the two actors gave a superb performance of 'thinking things over' and then announcing that they had decided to heed the advice from 'beyond' and stay with the show. Later, with a smile, they made it clear that they had already decided without any supernatural help. It served the production team right for resorting to these tactics!

Which is not to say that this does *not* happen in serious circumstances. It does, and often.

Such is the demand that Shirley MacLaine, the superstar of the psychic world, has cut back on her acting to pursue another career in this direction, offering help and passing on her accumulated occult wisdom. Other TV personalities are deeply and very sincerely interested in the paranormal and know a good deal about it. They include people like Michael Bentine and William Roache, whom we shall meet later.

Shirley Cheriton is a young actress who has already starred in a number of soaps, such as the hospital series *Angels*. In 1982 she worked on the children's educational series about space *The Final Frontier*, for which I spent some time putting together one of the programmes. Fred Talbot, who features later in the book (see p.155) was the host.

Soon afterwards, Shirley began work with the BBC on *EastEnders*, where she played Debbie Wilkins, and she was very popular with the viewers before her shock decision to quit in 1987. What led to that decision? She claims it was the advice of a psychic.

She was a little depressed, because her close friend Ross Davidson had been written out of the series (run over whilst saving a child), and her mind was toying with the idea of following suit and leaving the top-rated programme. Her visit to the psychic was partly to try to relieve this tension. Here she was told that a play would be offered and that it would be a big success. Also she would have a happy link with a man she was very fond of.

In fact, the play had already been offered at the time of the sitting and was scheduled to include Ross Davidson. This all helped to sway the decision, and Shirley made the wrench from the high-flying show. She does not appear to have regretted this move, although the play was not a particular hit.

Perhaps there is something about *EastEnders* that sends the cast scuttling towards psychics (quite possibly the rather morbid scripts!). Whatever the case, I found evidence that several other actors from this series consult psychics for advice. Of course, they rarely make this public. I would hazard a guess that it may well go on to a much greater degree, and with other soaps as well.

I did finally receive some assistance from the crew at

London's fictional Albert Square and was put through to Jon Padgen, who introduced himself as the astrological consultant to several members of the 'EastEnders' cast, notably Linda Davidson and June Brown (who plays the marvellous character of neurotic busybody, Dot Cotton).

June Brown agreed to participate in an experiment to test the merits of astrology. I procured a fancy computer program which, the instructions advised, was an aid to computation. You feed in the person's details and with a little bit of knowledge of how to manipulate its equations, you should end up with a unique reading for that particular subject. This was provided by the computer – more or less untouched by human hand – relying only upon the basic rules of astrology.

You might think that these rules would work if processed by a computer, irrespective of whether the world's greatest astrologer or a complete novice like me made the input. However, it is not quite as simple as that. A good deal of the skill in astrology comes from interpretation. That means the symbols of planetary movement (in this case pouring out of *my* computer) suggest key words and the human evaluator then decides which of these to keep or discard, to stress or underplay, and must blend and mix them together to make a report for the client.

None of these subtleties were possible in my experiment for, in this particular program, the machine makes the choice. So it was, in Jon Padgen's view, a necessarily flawed test. Nevertheless, I felt that if astrology had any merit then it ought to shine through such an objective examination. If it did not, then maybe people were just unconsciously accepting what they were told and treating the astrologer as a sort of psychic doctor, just as you would tend to believe your GP's prognosis of some illness and may even feel the symptoms they suggest you ought to have!

Part of June Brown's computer profile was, '... poetic and imaginative person, simple and creative tastes, who is very stable and dependable and ambitious'. How much of this was true and how much mumbo-jumbo was left up to June's judgement.

She thought that it was not as accurate as Jon Padgen's readings, a response we had both anticipated. And whilst there were points which compared with how she viewed herself, there were also problems.

The difficulty was that the computer had presented stark contrasts in her character. A professional (and human) astrologer such as Jon learns to blend these and, I suspect, offer the client a version that fits their own expectations. We all tend to believe the good news and reject the bad.

So I was not too surprised at only being judged around 50 per cent correct.

I did try it on another willing victim. The guinea pig on this occasion was BBC radio and TV personality Stuart Hall, probably best known internationally for his many years giggling through the loony equivalent of the Olympics, *'Jeux sans frontières'* or, as it was called in Britain, 'It's a Knockout'.

I was not prepared for the outcome of our little experiment.

From the start I could see that Stuart was impressed. 'There are several very accurate pieces in the computer's report,' he told me.

I asked if the success of the computer profile had surprised Stuart. His reply astonished me. 'I think it would have come as a big surprise, had I not had my horoscope cast for me by several professionals – mathematically minded people.' Stuart was another convert from the school of TV performers to the science of astrology.

'I think it's very good for you. It's like a sort of little catharsis. Somebody telling you exactly what they think of you, and you can't answer back,' Stuart noted.

In the end I asked for a score out of 100 for the computer's verdict and he was immediately prepared to offer 85 per cent. Of course, I was well aware that a predisposition in favour of the subject must colour any opinions. But Stuart Hall was very willing to argue lucidly in favour of the topic. 'I think astrology gives you a guideline. It makes you aware of your strengths and weaknesses ... If you take it to extremes and say I mustn't do this or that today, then astrology can be quite harmful. But I think if you allow it into your lives it can be helpful ...'

Anyone who has ever seen Stuart's (very natural) performances will know that he simply oozes merriment. He told me, 'My job is to make people happy. I think that's why I was placed on earth.' He gave me a prime example of this, fiddling with the computer print-outs in front of him and smiling so broadly you can practically hear it on my interview tape. 'It got one thing wrong here, though,' he said looking at the sheet. '... Ah, strong sex drive.' He pointed to where the computer highlighted this and chuckled: 'I have an *enormously* strong sex drive. One astrologer said to me, "Well there's no doubt about it, it's almost embarrassing this here".'

Our conversation was fast degenerating into hilarity, so Stuart concluded with the words of his human consultant: '... "The one thing about it is this ... He'll die in somebody's bed. But we're trying to find out whose".'

Another area I wanted to explore concerned predictions made for the future by showbusiness psychics. I had become intrigued when I visited a lady called Dorothy, who offered readings from a council house which the deafening noises all around indicated to be situated just off the end of the main runway into Manchester Airport. This was part of an entirely different experiment, not especially relevant to this book, although I was also researching soaps at the time – completely unknown to Dorothy.

In the midst of a flow of messages, the psychic suddenly slipped in the remark that I was going to be visiting somewhere. One word 'close', was stressed, and she insisted, 'Not an avenue or a road, but a close.' It meant nothing at the time, and she cannot have known (because I didn't know myself) that three weeks to the day later I would be invited to Liverpool to conduct an interview on 'The Close', as the scene of the Channel 4 TV soap *Brookside* is often called.

Another lady had already made her mark in the soap prediction stakes. She was also a housewife called Dorothy, but down the other end of the Mersey, in Liverpool.

I had come across Dorothy Wright in 1982 and 1983 when we worked with the same team at Radio City, a large, expanding station then fascinated by the listener-potential of the paranormal. We both ran series of features for some months.

Dorothy had come to the fore in an amazing way. In 1982 the football team Everton were in dire straits, languishing at the bottom of the league and losing everything in sight. Things were made far worse, because their neighbours, Liverpool, were just about the best team in the world. There was much despondency and talk of curses and jinxes, and Dorothy became convinced she could turn the tide.

Visiting Goodison Park, home of Everton FC, she used her ESP to sense what was wrong and then insist that the curse was driven out. Whether this was supposed to work in a psychological or spiritual manner is not very clear. Indeed, Dorothy, who is a very serious football fanatic (and supporter of rivals Liverpool!) went there only for a dare, she told me.

Either by virtue of something she did, or through pure coincidence, Everton Football Club never looked back. They have won almost everything that can be won since then and are no longer the underdogs to Liverpool. Dorothy said with a smile, when I interviewed her; 'I'm a bit sorry I bothered now!'

Nevertheless, this led to her fame spreading, and in 1986 and 1987 she was asked by the erstwhile magazine *Celebrity* to make predictions for the new year.

She told me about the psychic visions that occur: 'They just come to me in a flash. I get a picture in my mind, a bit like a photograph. Sometimes it symbolizes what is going to happen. Normally they work out, but it really bothers me when they don't come right.' On my reckoning about one-third do.

Her 1987 predictions included some very promising ones that did come right – at least, if some media reports are to be believed. She said, for example, that a rift would develop between the Prince and Princess of Wales. Other predictions completely fizzled out (thankfully including a suggestion that the White House would be bombed!). However, she had her most amazing successes with soap-opera characters.

Dorothy explained: 'I have often been consulted by TV personalities. Soap-opera characters in particular seem to find my advice a help. I think acting is a very superstitious profession anyway, and of course it's also a very precarious one.'

As to her 1987 predictions: 'I had to give these to the magazine some weeks before the end of 1986, and at the time they were really unexpected. They appeared in print on 1 January 1987 – long before the events took place.'

What events? Well, there were two in particular, based on favourite programmes about which she is often consulted.

For *EastEnders*, she said, 'A leading member of the cast will have a nervous breakdown and may even attempt suicide.' This was a staggering prediction which turned out to be horribly accurate. David Scarboro, the twenty-year-old actor who played the tearaway Mark Fowler, did indeed have a breakdown in the autumn of 1987. Series producer Julia Smith, interviewed at the time of the tragedy, said that it came as a complete shock to the cast and crew. David Scarboro entered a psychiatric ward for treatment but inevitably lost his job on the series.

On 6 January 1988 *Celebrity* reported this partial success for Dorothy's prediction. But fate was to take another hand. The story was still not over. A couple of weeks after publishing this 'success', Scarboro did try to commit suicide. The hysterical media had reported he was obsessed with the doomed life of fifties movie star James Dean, whom it was said the actor modelled himself upon. In April 1988, burnt out by all his problems, the *EastEnders* actor did end his life at the bottom of the sombre Beachy Head Cliffs, Britain's most notorious spot for suicide.[15]

Dorothy seemed genuinely sad when I asked her to comment on this. 'I was terribly upset about that. I saw it but could do nothing to prevent it. Even after he went into hospital, my prediction was carried in writing again and he still went ahead and died. It is very painful.'

Fortunately, her other 1987 prediction, whilst also a great shock, was not such a tragedy. She reported in January: 'I think Jean Alexander of *Coronation Street* may be written out of the series or she may ask to leave. I just sense that there are terrific question-marks about that character.'

To millions of viewers the world over, Jean Alexander, who played the charlady Hilda Ogden, *was Coronation Street*. She had been with the show since 1964 and was a British institution, having been given one of the highest acting awards for her performance. To suggest that she would quit was not merely ludicrous. It was heresy.

Dorothy Wright tells me how it happened: 'I saw Hilda's character getting a chopper, but I knew it was symbolic. Not that she would die, but that the character would be axed from the show. All year, after that prediction went in writing, people kept coming up to me asking "Come on, when is it going to happen?" – pretty well laughing at me and implying that it wouldn't. But I knew that it would.'

Six months after the prediction went into print, Jean Alexander approached her bosses at *Coronation Street* and asked to be written out of the show. She left at the end of the year. The move amazed everyone, including the TV production team, who tried hard to dissuade her. As Dorothy says, 'Nobody can argue with that one. I was spot on with a prediction that must be either psychic or an incredibly lucky guess.'

So what of her 1988 predictions? When you read this, you will know the truth, but as I write, the year is not yet over. Even so, there have been a couple of outstanding successes. In January she wrote that Liz Taylor would suffer ill health that would affect her work, and the week I spoke with Dorothy (in August 1988) it was revealed that Liz's acting future was very uncertain after reports of her needing major hip surgery.

Yet the biggest surprise of all came again from *EastEnders*. Dorothy explained that, 'Another cast member will suffer from so much pressure and exposure that she will leave the cast during 1988. I think that person will be Anita Dobson.'

Celebrity were so staggered by this news that they put it on the cover of their 6 January 1988 issue with the headline 'Anita To Quit'. Of course, it was vigorously denied at the time, but once again Dorothy was absolutely right. Anita Dobson, as important to *EastEnders* as Jean Alexander was to *Coronation Street*, and again ever-present in her role as Angie, the landlady of the Queen Vic pub, announced her decision in February 1988 and left the series a couple of months later.

One national newspaper, carrying the story on its front page, said: 'Anita Dobson is to leave *EastEnders*, it was revealed last night,' but added: 'She has been saying privately for some time that she will leave. The cast have known for a while that she won't be around for long.'[16]

Do we see here a clue to a way in which Dorothy Wright might have made an informed guess about this surprise move? After all, her biggest successes do seem to come in the field of soap operas, and she did tell me that various soap stars, whom she wouldn't name, had been her clients. I am not for one moment implying that Dorothy might be cheating, but ESP appears to rely upon obtaining information from the unconscious mind of a sitter.

What of 1989 and beyond? Dorothy seemed stuck on a most incredible claim that NASA had obtained proof of a strange form of alien life but were keeping it secret. She first reported this two years before, when she said the discovery occurred. But she is adamant that it has come to her so often in a vision that she has no doubt. 'The lifeform is very small. A bit like midges. It's not like us at all. They found it but are too scared to say so. But I am convinced this will be revealed by 1989.'

As for the soap operas, she had only one thing that stood out: 'I think Jean Alexander will soon regret her decision to leave *Coronation Street*. She will realize that viewers are fickle and a star can soon be forgotten. She will want to come back to the show.'

That is probably one prediction that millions of soap fans around the world will hope that 1989 really does make true.

Episode Three: The Outer Limits

Bob Monkhouse: Celebrity Scares

Now an internationally renowned entertainer, Bob Monkhouse began his career towards the end of World War II as a film cartoonist. He later became the master of topical one-liners and quips that led to scriptwriting work with the BBC and from there to his own shows, such as Celebrity Squares, Bob's Full House *and showcase talent series for newcomers.*

Soon after the war ended, the teenaged Bob was slaving day in, day out, over a table, creating wonderful cartoons. It was a long, arduous task matching each frame and making slight changes, so that when the whole thing was run together it would produce an impression of life.

All this went on in a small community created in a group of converted, very old houses just north of Maidenhead in Berkshire. It was a happy bunch of people, not averse to practical joking, but what happened one night in May 1946 was no joke.

Suddenly, Bob awoke shortly before 2 a.m. Later everyone else in the house confirmed that they had done the same. They knew the time because, moments after their waking in the cold, steely darkness of the quiet countryside, a large grandfather clock on the landing outside the bedrooms struck twice with its familiar chimes.

And then it began to rock from side to side.

Bob sat mesmerized in his bed, puzzled and yet unmoving. The sounds were now louder, and the clock seemed to be almost having convulsions as it swayed about. From the momentum, it was obvious that in seconds it would not only reach an apex and then swing back: its mass would carry it over and topple it onto the ground.

After a moment of frozen silence, this happened. The huge clock crashed to the ground at the top of the stairs and began to slide down them, with terrible shattering noises as it self-destructed. It hit base level with a crash. Then came the sounds of half a dozen people clattering out of their beds.

Bob expected to see the beautiful clock irreparably damaged at the foot of the stairs. But there was nothing there. The house was as it had been the night before.

All the occupants were accounted for. No one had seemingly been responsible. They all stood in astonishment, watching the grandfather clock ticking, as always, in its old familiar place.

I have heard this story from a number of sources, and the account has not varied. There is also a personal version, written by Bob Monkhouse himself in some detail.[17]

Of course, there are bound to be some chuckles that it was a grandfather *clock, bearing in mind the old song about the one that '... stopped – short – never to go again – when the old man died'. In fact, that song happens to be based on a number of real instances where favourite clocks have actually ceased at the exact moment of someone's death, as if a force from the beyond was attempting to communicate. The tale was told, for example, about the demise of the electronic genius Marconi.*

Jennifer O'Neill: Haunted by a Curse

Primarily a movie actress, Jennifer had a brief career as the star of a TV series, when in 1984 she made one run of Cover Up. *This adventure hokum was about a fashion agency getting mixed up in covert activities (spying, to you and me!) but was cut off in its prime by the culmination of the events to be described below.*

Jennifer O'Neill had lived with a curse for a very long time. Despite beauty queen looks that have guaranteed success, she has not had the happiest of times in her private life. Before the age of forty she had clocked up an incredible catalogue of half a dozen marriages, tragically failed pregnancies and serious accidents.

These ranged from the 'mundane' (falling off a horse

and severely injuring her back) to the 1982 near-catastrophe when she blasted herself in the stomach whilst loading a shotgun and had to undergo emergency, life-saving surgery. But these were merely the basis upon which her belief in a jinx was founded. One of her former husbands was murdered when gunmen burst into his New York offices to assassinate him with a hail of bullets.

Such was her pedigree when she made her big breakthrough, the TV series *Cover Up*. Jennifer knew that there would be dangerous stunts and gunfire. Of course, none of this was for real, but it was frightening none the less.

In most filming, for both movies and TV, an actor spends a great deal of the day 'between takes', waiting for the technicians to set up complex lighting and camera angles, or to put into motion the timing and precision that is required to perform a stunt. This tends to be even more commonplace on a series with as many plot contrivances as *Cover Up*.

During one such break Jennifer's co-star, who played a male agent with whom she shared romance and adventure, was playing with one of the toy guns. The term 'toy' is very misleading, for the guns were convincing and fired explosive emissions that gave off a great deal of noise and smoke, if not cold steel, but they were not considered dangerous, provided one handled them with circumspection and due reverence.

No one knows for sure what happened next. There were unconfirmed stories that the actor was playing 'Russian roulette' – just a single real pellet in the revolving case, with the odds stacked against its being the one that would emerge – this time, at least. Or it may have been a terrible accident.

Suddenly an explosion hit the room, and there was screaming. The gun had gone off whilst pointed straight at the TV star's head. He had died almost immediately. Jennifer O'Neill's tragic curse had struck again.

The series was in midstream, and they had to continue. American TV is all about advertising, and too much money was on the line to quit out of sentiment. But it was terribly difficult for Jennifer and the rest of the cast to force themselves back into work, and once commitments were over for the series, the programme was laid to rest with her co-star.

The scriptwriting was excellent as they accounted for the sudden disappearance of the actor. There was no abuse of the tragedy for popularity or ratings, and no sell-out, by packing him off to some fictional new life. Instead, without explanation, he was sent on a 'mission', out of camera, at the start of one episode. His return became overdue. As the episode closed, Jennifer was seen to ask 'When will he be coming back?' and was told, with real tears welling up in everyone's eyes, 'He won't be coming back.'

I missed something out from the account above – the name of the actor who died in that terrible misfortune. Jennifer's co-star was a bright young actor called Jon-Eric Hexum. 'Hex' is an ancient name for a spell or curse.

Pat Phoenix: Stranger in the House

When I was little, we moved from the Lancashire countryside to live in a two-up, two-down terraced house in the back streets of Rusholme, Manchester. It was a different world, and not one I was terribly fond of at the time. In 1960, when we had just bought our first very old and very tiny TV, a new series began to appear. At first it was to be called Florizel Street, *but it was renamed quickly when someone pointed out that this sounded a bit like a detergent. It emerged from the Granada workshops as* Coronation Street, *and many pundits gave it a few weeks' life-expectancy. After all, who would be interested in folk living in two-up, two-down terraced houses in the back streets of Manchester? Of course, they were, and 'the Street' has become the longest-running soap in Britain's TV history.*

In Victorian days, Sale was a village in Cheshire, about five miles south-west of Manchester and on the road to the high-class town of Altrincham (which most northern folk mispronounce as 'Altering 'em' and most southern folk consequently misspell as 'Altringham'). Its houses were large and grand, with rambling drives lined by impressive trees and gardens. They still are, of course, but Sale is now a commuter suburb with its homes owned by lawyers and accountants.

Pat Phoenix bought one of these herself, and it was here that she claims to have encountered just about the most famous ghost in show business. It is famous principally because so many people eventually saw it.

On the first occasion, it appeared to be nothing more than a woman who was carrying something in her hands (as if she was masking a candle, for example). Pat's dog had been alerted and pricked up its ears, causing her to glance up. The woman was so normal-looking that it never occurred to her that this could be a ghost. She followed the intruder through the door, got up and went after her. But, as you might imagine, no one was present. All that remained was a strange coldness, as if the temperature had leaked from the room through an invisible hole.

After that Pat began to see the woman often. Despite the fact that she was ordinary and solid, it quickly became apparent that she was a phantom. For a start, she wore her hair in an old-fashioned bun and had a long grey dress that she wore all the time. The apparition manifested in different parts of the house (even the garden) and was always in this action-replay mode, walking with the object in her hands. She was never heard to speak. Nor did she appear to know that anyone else was present. Yet there was no animosity there. Nothing was frightening about the spectre at all.

Several members of the ITV production team visited the house and either saw the rather elderly woman or heard strange noises (bumps and bangs coming from the ceiling). Always, when she was visible, she would vanish when the observer's eyes were turned away, as if the very act of switching attention caused the vision to be disturbed.

After making discreet enquiries, Pat discovered that the house had once been owned by an old dear named Madame Mueller. She became convinced this was the ghost. Her description fitted, and there were reasons why this woman might be 'in tune' with the TV star. Both loved animals, and Mrs Mueller had been an actress in her day too. Retirement had seen her fall down on her luck and have to scrape a living together as the end drew near.

That Pat Phoenix was the focus for this ghostly encounter may be linked with her belief in ESP, plus the significant fact that Mrs Mueller also once turned up in the other Phoenix household (a flat in the city centre, nearer the TV studios). In other words, the spook was somehow dependent upon Pat Phoenix in order to manifest. But you either choose to take this as meaning that it was an externalization of Pat's intuitive knowledge of and affinity with the memory of the actress, or that the old lady's spirit was being drawn to her successor.

In 1986 I was just about to arrange for Pat Phoenix to tell her story on a radio programme I put together about ghosts when she became very ill with cancer. She fought bravely against it, spending time in a large private hospital in Cheadle. As the end approached, she married her long-time friend, actor Tony Booth, at her bedside. Then she slipped away.

Her interest in the paranormal was sparked by her ghostly experiences. This turned her into another admirer of Doris Stokes, who had visited her in hospital. After her death, the Manchester Evening News *called Doris to pass on the news. She was then bombarded with calls from other newspapers, intruding on her sorrow with only one interest. Had Doris established contact with the deceased TV star?*

'They didn't really want a tribute. They wanted to know if Pat had come back to talk to me,' Doris understandably bemoaned. But, as she pointed out, it was not possible to find Pat Phoenix in some post-mortem directory and give her a call with a psychic telephone.

However, the next day (when the newspapers had given up their hunt for a story) Pat did 'turn up' out of the blue. She asked Doris to phone Tony Booth at home, convey the news that Pat was OK and ask him to keep the ring that she had married him with. He did, placing it on a chain round his neck. Maybe Pat is now reunited with Doris Stokes and Madame Mueller.

Gordon Piper: A Country Poltergeist

If you listen to the TV pundits, they will tell you that there are two really terrible kinds of programme: endless American game shows and Australian soap operas. Nevertheless, both keep the audiences watching, and afternoons would be unthinkable for many viewers in Great Britain without regular excursions into family life Down Under.

I work most days, of course, so (fortunately?) miss all these, but the late-night escapades of the inmates of Wentworth Detention Centre in Melbourne, as portrayed in Prisoner *(a series that ran from 1978 to 1986) have attracted new admirers, including me, even though most of the prisoners and staff seem to have been incarcerated for their acting ability.*

Of all of the daytime shows, only one exercises my video recorder on a regular basis and is worthy of the prime-time slot British moguls deny it. A Country Practice *is set in a rural community and is a bit like* Emmerdale Farm *in atmosphere, although with the rare asset of good scripts and pleasant characters. It combines elements from medical dramas, even much of the appeal of the James Herriot 'country vet' stories, and rarely destroys its lightness with the kind of doom and gloom some British soaps seem to find inescapable, or the ludicrous storylines and over-acting that the American equivalent could hardly do without.*

Since it began in 1980, A Country Practice *has churned out an hourly episode twice a week and, since Britain shows it at only half that rate, it is sliding into a mysterious time-warp of the programme-planners' making.*

Gordon Piper has been a stalwart of the show throughout, playing Bob Hatfield, the handyman cum odd-job person. It's not really a role that has an equivalent in British society (unless you count Benny in Crossroads *– and there is little similarity!), but the fact that he can exist as an anachronism in the late eighties shows the endurance and appeal of these tales from the people of Wandin Valley. It reminds me of my roots in Lancashire's Rossendale Valley, where many of the characters that come to life on screen really did exist.*

It started in the living-room. Gordon was suddenly disturbed by his dog barking loudly. This was not like Charlie. She never made a din in the house.

Clambering up to watch, with bemusement Gordon saw her rush over towards the bedroom (which is on the same level), still yapping as if caught up by some invisible presence. The door was shut, and she stood there peering with eyes aflame as if pleading to be let into the room and reach the intruder.

Gordon reacted swiftly but cautiously. He teased the door open, wondering if someone might have entered unseen and unheard. Charlie brushed past and clattered around the bed to approach the wardrobe and sit by it, still barking. Now it seemed obvious. Someone *had* to be in the closet. Gordon walked towards it, figuring that whoever it was would be frightened enough by now. He grabbed the handle and wrenched it open.

The wardrobe was empty of all but clothes. The moment this fact was revealed to them both, Charlie stopped barking and went back about her business as if nothing had happened.

That night Gordon's wife cooked a splendid supper, and they used a fine Wedgwood china dinner-service that had been a wedding present from an elderly aunt. It is used for special treats and, as always, was washed with great care and then put away in the cupboard. Because of the size and shape of this storage space, it is only possible to put the dinner service in one way. Once in, it fits snugly and cannot be manoeuvred around.

They went to bed, leaving nothing but an upturned drinking-glass to drain beside the sink.

In the morning things were not the same. His first glance in the kitchen told Gordon that. The glass was now the right way up, as if it had been used again. Next to it were a cup, saucer and plate from the Wedgwood service, as if someone had been in overnight and helped himself.

Gordon went to ask his wife why she had got up in the middle of the night and also why she had used the best china, when it would have been her normal practice to have left that well alone. No one else was in the house, so it had to be her doing.

She was just about to ask him the same question. She had assumed that Gordon had been the culprit.

Dismissing the argument as just one of those things that happens from time to time, they resigned themselves to putting the good dishes back into their safe resting-place in the cupboard. But when they opened it, there was quite a shock.

The Wedgwood service was perfectly intact, but it had been rotated to fit in at an angle that was aesthetic but which they had never been able to achieve. They looked at one another in astonishment. Not only had someone taken their crockery but they had succeeded in replacing it in a unique way.

These events occurred in 1981, soon after the TV series began. Gordon was not upset. There were no tensions in the house. It was just a curious, isolated and unexplained event.

For years afterwards, until this story was related to me, Gordon and his wife tried to place the dinner service in the cupboard at that same angle. They have never succeeded and still believe it to be quite impossible.

But someone – or something – knows how.

Many people have something like this happen in their home. Later you will read about weird events in the life of Doreen Sloane. You might imagine that there are perfectly ordinary explanations, but, as in this case, they are rarely very obvious.

The questions that pose themselves are, of course, did Gordon or his wife use the crockery during the night without remembering? Was Charlie's barking a coincidence or, as many believe, was she merely demonstrating the increased sensitivity that animals possess?

The word 'poltergeist' sums up what this was – an invisible force that moves objects about with no evident purpose or design. Not that this explains a thing about what a poltergeist might be! Theories range from temper tantrums of the subconscious mind to hauntings by immature spirits, or the return of the favourite aunt eager to suggest a new way of storing her dinner service.[18]

William Roache: The Cosmic Student

William Roache was born in Derbyshire, spent several years in the army, until he left at the rank of captain, and has been an actor for over thirty years. But he is known almost exclusively for his television part as a Lancashire man from the fictional town of Weatherfield. He is, in fact, the last original survivor of Britain's longest-running soap opera, Granada TV's Coronation Street.

He began his role as Ken Barlow, in the opening episodes of 1960, when a young and rebellious student; Ken has gone through several incarnations and marriages since then. In some respects, Ken Barlow is seen as a bit of an old stick-in-the-mud who rarely does anything adventurous or unexpected. William Roache, on the other hand, could not be so described, for his interest and involvement in the paranormal is quite extensive. He has also done little to hide it, and many people are aware that he has some occult leanings, although they may not fully appreciate the extent to which these go.

He kindly granted me a short interview between rehearsals, amidst the heavy pressures of producing two episodes per week. This is a show that attracts 20 million viewers in Britain alone, is seen in many overseas countries and has even received praise from the Queen's poet laureate.

William Roache is a deeply religious man. But his religion is much more broadly based than simple Christianity.

He admits that he once turned away from the Church because he became disillusioned with what it had to offer. There was too much petty squabbling about matters of dogma. He also felt that so-called men of peace sometimes behave in a far too angry manner and that real peace can only begin with the individual. It is necessary to nurture this and allow it to grow, so that violence will be stifled through a natural process. He believes that many things can be learned from other religions, particularly Eastern doctrines, because these offer clues about the nature of the universe which are incompatible with basic Christianity.

It was in this quest to look beyond basic Christianity to

see what other philosophies had to offer that he became involved with the paranormal. 'It was a learning process,' he told me. 'I regard myself as a cosmic student. I am continuously discovering new things and realize that there is still so much to learn.'

He likens this process, which has gone on over many years, to a personal search for the 'Holy Grail': 'Only the people who study the paranormal can really comprehend what there is to understand about it. You need to enquire, and keep enquiring, until you build up a store of knowledge and information. This in turn brings with it realization of the ultimate truths.'

Perhaps his most unusual studies (to add to astrology and UFOs) come with his increasing acceptance of the reincarnation principle. He believes that after death we do not simply languish in an ethereal heaven, but are born again and return to live afresh on this earth. 'All people are immortal and live more than once in a physical sense,' he assured me.

'I think you should research with an open mind,' he said. 'But you must not be credulous. People either have a very closed-minded opinion when it comes to these subjects, or else they open up their arms and accept everything. Neither of those positions is the correct one, in my view. You should explore, but you should do so with caution.'

William has deep feelings about those who do this and suffer as a consequence. He has little tolerance for the newspaper or, perhaps surprisingly, the TV presentation of the paranormal. 'The media cannot handle this subject properly,' he complains. 'They just want to make it sensationalist and fun. Yet there is so much more to it than that, if only they could see. You just cannot talk to them on the correct level. Not in the way they would treat other sober issues. You talk to them about astrology as a serious field, and what happens? They dismiss it as nonsense and star signs. They either will not look, or simply are not capable of looking, deeper into what the paranormal stands for and implies.'

'I become very perturbed when I see people dismissing Prince Charles,' William acknowledges. 'I know him to be a wonderful and a sincere man. Yet because of his reasonable and honest interest in the paranormal he becomes the subject of unfair attacks. To be associated with it in any way is tantamount to being proclaimed a "loony", in some people's eyes.'

He concluded: 'As a society we need to learn to remove ourselves from such rigid lines of thought. We have to try and accept that the paranormal is a subject that is rich in things that are there to be understood. To me all of this is better than a novel. The truth about the paranormal is more exciting than any fiction.'

Cliff Robertson: Please Don't Go!

Born in the sunshine of La Jolla, California, in 1925, Cliff Robertson has appeared in TV series since the good old days of The Twilight Zone, *but he has also had a brilliant career on the stage and in movies, including the rare honour of an Oscar for his superb portrayal of a mentally retarded man in the 1968 film* Charly.

Cliff entered the world of soap through the part of Dr Michael Ranson in the very successful tale of California vineyards Falcon Crest.

After his parents died whilst he was still young, Cliff was raised by his grandmother. She cheered him on as he rose through the actors' school in New York and moved to Broadway with bit-parts in shows.

Just after the war, that special bond still existed between them, even though the grandmother was 3,000 miles away, back home in La Jolla, and Cliff was taking a break in the lakeland area of New Hampshire where he was then in a play. He rented a small cottage and drank in the fresh air of the chilled but inviting wind.

Then came the nightmare.

It struck in the middle of the night, around 3 a.m., and the focus was his grandmother. Cliff dreamed that she was telling him that her life was over. It had been a long one and he must not cry. It was just time to go. Cliff pleaded with her, but she insisted. She was ready. All was at peace. There was nothing to worry about. The debate stretched on as the nightmare continued. Finally, his grandmother shook her head and said, 'Very well.' She agreed to try not to leave.

The actor awoke in a sweat. The darkness of the night smothered him but could not blot out the terror of his nightmare. It had been just a dream, he told himself. But it seemed so powerful and real.

There was no phone in the isolated house, but a return to sleep was impossible. He considered going into town, but it was now almost 4 a.m. and with the three-hour time-difference that was still the early hours of the morning in California. He walked up and down in turmoil.

At 6.30 a knock sounded on his door. There stood a sheepish youngster from the theatre, holding a telegram. Cliff's heart pounded. As he tore open the envelope, he could only fear the worst. It was from his aunt back in La Jolla, who reported that his grandmother was very ill. With the dream from just hours before still etched in his mind, he went back into town and called right away. The illness had struck at midnight California time. The old lady had collapsed and the doctor had rushed over. By the time he arrived, she was dying. He offered little hope to the distraught aunt, and she had immediately sent the telegram, hoping that Cliff might be able to fly home and see his grandmother one last time.

But then, shortly afterwards as the night wore on, Cliff's grandmother had suddenly grown stronger. She rallied and fought through the critical period. Now, as dawn was set to break in California and Cliff sat by the phone in mid-morning New Hampshire, the prognosis was much brighter. The doctor was amazed.

She did pull through. Cliff Robertson is convinced that it was his dream self pleading with her to stay which made all the difference. He had communed with her spirit across the breadth of a continent and in doing so may have saved her life.

There are many stories just like this. Any researcher of the paranormal is familiar with them. Indeed, I would venture to say that what are called 'crisis apparitions' are just about the most common form of ESP there is.

The theory goes that in times of great stress the mind sends out a distress signal and is bonded by the huge emotion of that moment with someone close to them. However, that other person would normally repel all psychic boarders. We have a kind of shield that we place in front of the conscious mind, denying entry of such raw, preconscious ESP messages.

Something else has to happen to raise the drawbridge and let them through. The mind of the receiver has to alter its state of consciousness. If this happens when the receiver is awake, the essence of the incoming message might be projected onto the real world as a vision. This is just the mind's dramatic way of grabbing attention. What Cliff Robertson saw was not the 'ghost' of the grandmother come to visit but a pictorial representation of her conjured up by his own memory, to illustrate the news that his deep subconscious mind was receiving.

However, for most people (as here) an easier way to receive ESP input is in the natural altered state of consciousness that each one of us enters for a third of every day – sleep. Then the dramatization occurs not in the real world of the bedroom but in a dream. Yet the principle is the same.

The question unanswered by all of this is whether Cliff's grandmother was also tuned in to him and so decided not to die, because of what he told her. Or did Cliff simply detect her own fight against the illness and the tremendous will she had to survive, illustrating this in his dream as the conversation that determined her destiny?

I leave the choice up to you.

Jean Rogers: The Power of Love

Seeing the character of Dolly Skilbeck on Yorkshire TV's Emmerdale Farm, you very likely would expect certain things of the actress who has filled that role since 1980. You might imagine a sort of Pennine ruggedness, the hardiest of virtues chiselled out by her broad dialect. Also you would doubtless *picture a woman who lives a simple life, tending farm animals and looking after a ponderous husband and young child. But, in fact, you would be a long way from the truth. The reality of Jean Rogers shatters most of those illusions. Behind Dolly there lies a very pleasant and intelligent person who can talk volubly about strange phenomena, based on both her personal experience and her sensible reading of many books. Yet she tempers this with a seldom found, yet often needed, blend of deep spiritual and Christian feelings, for this is also a mind that see dangers in the paranormal, stalking in the bushes that line the highway through life.*

Even Jean Rogers' past is far removed from the Yorkshire Dales, as you immediately realize on hearing her refined, BBC-approved accent. She was born in Middlesex, raised by the sea in Sussex (still her favourite place for relaxation) and even now has ties to the area. Before taking on the challenge of becoming the 'new' Dolly, a metamorphosis very uncommon in British soaps, she had appeared in other series, including the now forsaken Crossroads, *but was perhaps best noted for her presentation of and her writing of material for the ever-popular BBC radio series* Listen with Mother, *on which British children were weaned in the days before videos and computer games. It seems almost an anachronism to place Jean's lively modern approach to the supernatural alongside the world of children's characters, but it also provides the homely feel, which may be important in allowing her to work the magic on our TV screen – magic necessary in order that she become a person who, in truth, she is not much like. But, of course, as we have seen, this capacity is what makes an actor an actor, and what also opens up the mind and the emotions to wondrous paranormal mysteries.*

When Jean auditioned for *Emmerdale Farm*, it could not have come at a more dreadful time.

Emmerdale, as she affectionately calls it, had been clawing its way through the ratings since 1972, being scattered round the schedules by the indifferent regions in a haphazard, slipshod fashion that left it fighting an uphill battle. The appointment of a new actress for the role of Dolly towards the end of 1979 was seen as a vital ingredient in future plans, as she was to be a central character in the years to come.

Over fifty actresses were up for the part. It was a bit like ITV's equivalent of the *Gone With The Wind* selection of the actress to portray Scarlett O'Hara. Eventually there was a short list of six, and Jean, to her surprise, was on it.   But then tragedy struck out of the blue. Her mother, to whom she was devoted, passed away. It was mid December, and only one final interview remained. It was now make or break. The part meant a great deal to her, but Jean could focus on nothing but her mother. When the last interview was innocently set for the day of the funeral, it seemed like fate. There was never any question in Jean's mind which one she would attend.

'So far as I was concerned, the interview wasn't important,' she explained. 'I thought, if they really want to see me, they can do it any other day.' But, as it happened, her father, perhaps recognizing that this was a terrible dilemma for his daughter, chose to alter the date of the funeral and so make both things possible.

With Christmas approaching, the question of music to play at the service became important. Jean remembers: 'As a kid, I used to visit the Worthing music festival. My favourite was the carol "Silent Night", sung in German. But my mother's favourite carol was called "Brightest and Best". I decided that I wanted these to be played at the memorial.'

It meant making changes to the accompaniment, which was not geared up to handle carols, but Jean felt so strongly in her mind that her mother would want it that she paid for the alterations herself. 'I can remember singing my heart out, thinking, "Thank you, God, for a lovely mum" and "This one is for you." The week after Christmas, in church, they again played "Brightest and Best", and I cried my eyes out.'

As 1980 began, she learnt that she had got the job in *Emmerdale*. She was to travel north to Leeds to meet the cast then involved in the storyline. 'All the way north from Shepperton,' Jean says, 'I could not stop thinking about my mother. Throughout that first day I was saying to myself. "Wouldn't it be nice if mum could see this." '

With these thoughts buzzing in her mind, she met the actors who would be her working partners for years to come. In one free moment she was showing off a pendant when an actress who had a small part in the current episodes but who was not a regular in the series came over to Jean and asked to hold the item. 'I feel I have to say something to you,' she announced, to everyone's surprise, not least that of Jean herself.

This actress was practising what Jean now knows to be called 'psychometry', the ability to read someone's emotions or impressions simply by holding an object with close associations. It is not unlike dowsing in the way in which it operates.[19]

The actress 'read' three things from the pendant. First, she saw a large room with big windows, letting in much light yet somehow empty and with great loneliness. In the window a cat was sitting all on its own. This Jean recognized as a good description of her home and cat (which she had named Kismet, an old word for 'fate'). But, as she said to me, 'I thought, maybe there's something in it, maybe not. This woman could have heard about my mother's death somewhere and imagined the rest.'

But the other things offered were more specific. The actress now spoke of Jean's mother: 'Don't worry. I have to tell you that she is very happy. You need only think of her and she is here.' That seemed remarkable, considering Jean's overwhelming but unspoken, desire that her mother should see this day of triumph.

Finally, the impromptu psychic reading ended with the statement that, 'Music is important', and it was music in the sense of performance not of playing. This baffled Jean, because her mother had never been especially involved with music. She shrugged the comments off as of no significance.

'I thought about this,' Jean told me. 'I felt it was comforting to know my mother was there. It did no harm and, if it was true, then at least she knew about *Emmerdale*, was very happy and was still with me.'

Yet the uncertainties remained as she returned south that evening. It had been a strange day, but the whole thing might well be nothing more than a combination of wishful thinking and coincidence.

And then, out of the blue, a thought came sailing as if

from nowhere. 'It came entered my mind. I just knew that Mum was saying, "Thank you for the music at the funeral." '

With this conviction still fresh in Jean's awareness, another twist was to occur the following morning. Back in London she was with her father. He was a complete agnostic who would barely suffer the paranormal at all, but he said over breakfast: 'You know, at about 3 a.m. this morning I suddenly got this feeling that your mother had her arms around me.' Jean explained to me that this sort of demonstrative behaviour was uncharacteristic. But it had made its impression on her father. 'He said, "It's silly, isn't it? It was almost as if she was making sure we were all right." '

The fact that the two events had taken place within hours of one another, and both on the day of the 'reading' in Leeds, helped persuade Jean that there was more than chance behind them. 'I thought it was important. I asked myself why it happened to me then, at that time. And it all seemed so clear.'

This was just the start of things. On several occasions since, Jean has been approached by sensitives who have wanted to pass on messages from her mother – '... to let me know that she is still there watching me'. As she is a deeply religious person, this created some difficulties for Jean.

'How can I equate this as a Christian? At times when I have been in an emotional hiatus, these messages would find their way to me. I would never pay to go and see someone. They just reached me. Yet, even though they are done with love, they still have that stamp of my mother's personality. I find this comforting because, although there are a lot of questions you can ask, I think we are still here to work out our own destiny. There is a danger in receiving these messages. You can think that you are channelling into something beyond you and that you will receive all the answers to everything. Life is not like that. I think life's a process of learning.'

Eventually, Jean was able to incorporate these messages into her spiritual views. She has even preached about this sort of thing in church. 'I tell them that now I can understand what Christ says in the Bible when He explains how love is very powerful. Death does not stop love.'

Even so, she risks the dangers. 'One has to be careful. If you dwell on the bad things, it can be harmful. Not everything that passes over is good.'

I told her about Johnny Caesar's experience, and this led to a discussion about ouija boards and spirit contact.

'That game was banned,' she said, with evident relief. 'I would never touch a ouija board. It's very bad, especially for kids. They are vulnerable to that sort of influence.'

Nevertheless, she was not pessimistic: 'Basically, if you believe that the strongest of all things is love – and love is good – you are able to put the rest in perspective.'

She has now learnt more about her own inner potential through reading books by psychics such as Doris Stokes and Shirley McLaine, although, when we discussed some of the latter's ideas in more detail, it was clear Jean could not take them all on board. 'She leaves me when she goes on about UFOs. It's just that my credibility is over-stretched. But, having said that, it may be that I'm just not ready to take it. It just seems too interfering – something coming from beyond Earth like that.'

She has less trouble with other esoteric ideas: 'I can accept something like reincarnation much more readily, because it explains many things that I find puzzling about people. You can meet someone I would call a "refined soul" and others who are not – yet their background, their age and so on do not seem to have anything to do with it. I feel it could be that they have experienced more another time, and they come back with that and have a head start.'

I reminded Jean of lines in the Bible where Jesus asked whether it was the blind man or his father who had sinned in order that he be born blind. She had not seen this as relevant, having assumed that it meant a birth defect caused by the father's sin. But the point which seems to support reincarnation is that Jesus quite comfortably embraced the option that the man himself *might* have sinned before his birth in order to cause his blindness. How could he, unless he had existed beforehand, unless he had lived before?

'Jesus never actually said that previous lives were not true,' Jean admitted. 'He certainly does not refute any of it. What the Bible says most of the time is that we should dwell in the light.'

By tuning herself to accept the paranormal, Jean has found that her sensitivities have been enhanced. She now believes that she can sense atmospheres.

'The only way I can pinpoint is when I go round to look at a house,' she notes. 'I just *feel*. But how do I *know*? It creates a reaction within me.

She searched for a way to elaborate. 'Take the house I am in now. In no way do I feel threatened by it, yet, having said that, when I bought it, it needed much decoration. I felt very, very strongly that it had been neglected. Yet, as soon as I put the paint on, it was as if the house had sighed and settled back to relax.'

Jean looked at me as if I would find this concept preposterous, but it is all part of psychic sensitivity. Reading atmospheres like this is no different from psychometry on a pendant or using a twig to say where water is buried.

Obviously encouraged, she went on: 'I remember visiting a house at Shepperton – I suppose it was about sixty years old. The place was so unhealthy. There was something fundamentally wrong with it. It's like you can stand next to someone who is really ill and, even if you can see nothing, there is just something about it. I respond emotionally. You know how smells can do it. The smell of coffee grinding and I am back in Worthing, eight years old.'

I wondered if this same sensitivity extended to living things. Jean confirmed that it did: 'I pick up from people all the time. Sometimes I rather wish I didn't, because it can unsettle me. I think it has something to do with me, whereas, in fact, it is just their mood I am picking up. I am better with strangers, really, because then I know it isn't me. I can instantly "know" what to say when I am removed from the situation.'

I told her how, in researching this book, I was discovering just how many actors possessed this ability and that I believed it tied in with the way ESP is at heart an emotional message. She instantly saw my point.

Jean remarked that ghosts may well exist through this very simple capacity: 'Often they are seen at the place where somebody has died in a tragic way and there has been a lot of emotion left behind. I am fascinated by how you can visit churches and, to me, some seem so empty when others are just full. The walls are alive with human emotions.' Jean paused to clarify her thoughts: 'It's extraordinary. I guess it is just being able to tell whether the vibes are right or not.'

I told her the story of actress Susannah York who, when looking for a new house in Essex, felt she had found one that looked perfect. It even had a drawbridge over a moat. But on both occasions she visited it she sensed something wrong – an atmosphere, a 'bad vibe'. On the second occasion, staying at night, she practically collapsed with the overpowering feeling that someone had died after jumping into the moat when the bridge became stuck. The estate agent had to confirm that this really had occurred.

Maybe ghosts are nothing more than images from the past picked up as raw emotions and transformed beyond simple feeling into a visual image. It may merely depend upon how creative are the senses to the percipient. Some just *feel* the ghost as a mood or sensation; others *hear* it as a spectral noise or see it as a full-blown vision.

This awareness that the overlap between paranormal and normal may well be an illusion has left Jean Rogers a little bothered by the sceptics and the myth-makers. She is also concerned that not enough scientists are willing to look at what is really going on.

'Within science, things vary a lot. But more and more the scientists are having to keep an open mind. Eventually they have to go back to what we call God to help explain things. Look at Black Holes. Within our concept of three dimensions, it is totally impossible to imagine something that can invert on itself and become endless.' Yet, despite lessons such as these, scientists do not always learn from them, she fears. 'People who go into science are searching with a great belief that they are going to get all the answers, but, I believe, the more you know, the more you realize what you don't know.'

She hates the way the paranormal is abused: 'Why do they call it "the occult" in libraries? That to me spells disaster. It really angers me, because it makes me think of witchcraft. But the things I have experienced come from the spirit of love going on, and that is perfectly fine for me as a Christian. But others still look at me, because of these labels, and say, "Ooh, you are dabbling in the occult." '

Even so, she agrees that there are dangers. 'When you try to organize it or teach it, it can be. I accept that it is important to spread what is happening, but not everybody is ready. It is like with children when they start asking questions. The danger is that you start to tell them too much and they cannot cope with it.'

This reminded her of an experience she recently had with her young daughter.

'It was about two in the morning. I awoke and looked at the bedroom door and saw the handle turn – or I *feel* it did. The door just seemed to bulge. So I said, "Yes, hello. Justine?" Somehow I was convinced it was her. It was so real. I felt awake. Next day I questioned her, and she said that she had not tried to come in. But I asked about her dreams, and she had been very scared in one at that time. I felt that, perhaps, she had become so frightened and wanted me that she projected her thoughts into my room.'

Whether this is what happened or whether that is pure speculation remains difficult to say, but when someone can empathize with another to the extent that they can sense their moods and thoughts, it is not out of the question that fear and anxiety could transmit themselves from daughter to mother. In a dream state, that fear might be transformed into a vivid and realistic paranormal experience, a drama that spells out the desire. In the mind? Well, certainly it would be, but that is precisely where all psychic phenomena seem to begin and end.

Harry Secombe: A Spectre in the Audience

After World War II four young ex-servicemen got together. According to one of them, Michael Bentine, whom we have already met, they were so astonished that they had survived the war that their natural exuberance poured out in zany comedy. They formed a team called 'The Goons' and dominated radio and then TV in the forties and fifties. But they were all multi-talented. Aside from Michael, there was Spike Milligan, who is still a noted wit, and Peter Sellers, who became a movie legend, in particular for his immortal role as Inspector Clouseau in the Pink Panther *films. And then there was Harry Secombe, who matured from comedy to become an internationally renowned singer but who is also the long-standing host of the spiritually uplifting TV roadshow* Highway.

As we have already seen, Britain is littered with haunted theatres. In London, the most famous must be the Theatre Royal in Drury Lane. Many spooks are reputed to stalk the boards there. One is Dan Leno, a Victorian comedian who was a great star but burnt himself out very young and died in tragic circumstances.

In a previous book I reported on the remarkable experiences of entertainer Roy Hudd who has made a special study of 'music hall' and of Leno in particular. Hudd had a series of weird dreams that seemed to preview an eventual chance visit to the London home in which his predecessor had practised his craft. This uncanny 'premonition' ensured Roy Hudd's fascination with the man.[20]

Whether it was Leno's ghost that has been seen on many occasions by actors and audiences at the Theatre Royal is not always clear. In some cases, the identification has been made; in others it remains more vague, and ghost-hunter Andrew Green refers to the Drury Lane phantom as 'the man in grey'.[21]

About twenty years ago Harry Secombe was appearing at the Theatre Royal in the light-hearted musical *The Four Musketeers*, loosely based on the famous novel by Alexandre Dumas. He reports an experience in his dressing-room when he and the man responsible for his wardrobe were suddenly startled by a shaking amidst the coathangers: they swung violently about from side to side.

Of course, one might speculate about tube trains passing below, but, although this does effect certain parts

of London, the Theatre Royal is not especially afflicted –
besides which, there were also strange tapping noises on
the wood of the wardrobe at the same time.

Harry Secombe had little doubt about the nature of this
'poltergeist', because he and other members of the cast
also saw the apparition on one occasion.

It is typically described as little more than a grey light
that shines with a fuzzy sort of opaqueness and moves
about the stage set. The history of the theatre records
instances where hundreds of people at once supposedly
saw this thing.

*Regular appearances by ghosts are known as 'hauntings'. Some
say that a kind of 'emotional fingerprint' is left behind by
someone very fond of a particular venue. No intelligent being
returning from death is needed in this theory, just a sort of
perpetual replay of a video-tape.*

Simon Slater: Fitting the Bill

*Simon Slater is a dashing young actor who was once best known
for his role in a popular TV advert, in which he played a British
Airways steward who turned into 'Superman' to get passengers
out of tricky situations. In the autumn of 1987 he joined the cast
of the hard-hitting police series* The Bill, *although his role as a
Yuppie inspector was not carried over in the summer of 1988
when* The Bill *was turned into a twice-weekly and more
traditional soap.*

In the early hours of 20 September 1987 I awoke with
sweat pouring out of me. I had just suffered a terrible
nightmare. Not that this is particularly unusual. Yet this
dream was drenched with emotion, and I knew the signs.
When that happens, it suggests something paranormal.

In the dream I had seen a man beside a lake or pond. I
knew that he had been given a 'dare' to wade into it and
was gingerly stepping out and immersing himself in the
dark waters. I could sense that he felt he was showing off
by doing this, although he appeared to be prodding

around as if looking for something that had been submerged.

Then suddenly disaster struck. He was trapped. I could see him struggling to move about, and sense the thick mud on the bottom of the pond that was oozing all around him. The harder he struggled, the worse it became. He tried to free himself, but it was no use. I was only able to gaze on helplessly through my dream eyes as this unknown man sank ever deeper and drowned. The nightmare came to its fitful conclusion as the flashing lights of police vehicles appeared and the cars parked beside the lake.

That Sunday I pondered this dream. It seemed very real, and I felt sure that it related to an event that might well happen. I have had a number of powerful dream precognitions like this before, and I can tell them apart from normal fantasies. That is why I scribbled down a few notes on these images and wondered. I did not know the man and had no possible way of preventing any tragedy – if, indeed, it was a preview of a real event and not just my imagination.

On Monday 21 September, Thames TV screened the first of the new episodes of *The Bill*. No bells rang or lights flashed as I watched it. Simon Slater joined the cast that day as an arrogant upper-crust copper.

As part of the promotion for the top-rated series, this new actor was a natural asset, so he was widely interviewed. In one interview he related the story of his first week of filming.

Simon's character, Brian Kite, was instantly disliked by his East London colleagues because of his upper-class accent and attitudes, so the plot of one episode (not the first to be transmitted when the editing was completed) saw them pull a practical joke on him. He received top-secret instructions to go to the River Thames and collect mud samples. The joke note said there was danger of toxic pollution. Believing all this, the inspector went, without telling anyone, and waded out, getting himself very messy in the process. His samples were totally useless, of course.

But there was more to it than this. Slater admitted that

he had almost died during the filming of the scene. Although you would never guess this from the calm presentation on screen, he had suddenly found himself sinking deeper and deeper into thick slime. It sucked him into the bottom of the river like quicksand, and within moments he was swallowed up to the waist in mud and dirty water. He plunged lower, realizing in split seconds of panic that he was in real danger of drowning. He yelled out for help, as the water closed in on him; a rope was thrown down and he was hauled to safety. It was, he said, '... one of the most terrifying experiences I have ever had. ... I will never forget it as long as I live.'[22]

I was astonished by these revelations. There is no way I could have known about them on the night of 19/20 September 1987, and could it really be coincidence that this was just a day before *The Bill* reappeared on TV or that I was then deeply immersed in compiling stories for this book, asking actors about the strange phenomena in their lives?

My dream seemed to be remarkable. It really does fit the bill.

I accept that this case does not fit into this book's pattern. This is not really a spooky experience by an actor in a TV soap. But it most certainly was a very spooky experience about an actor in a soap, and if it is a genuine paranormal dream, then Simon Slater presumably had some role in it.

What explanations can there be? Coincidence, perhaps? I find this very unlikely. The details of my dream match so exactly those in Simon Slater's real experience that it stretches credulity to call it fortuitous – particularly with my association with this book at that time.

Of course, my dream was not a literal reproduction of the event (which had already happened when I dreamt it, so it was a precognition of my discovery of the incident, not the incident itself). The actor was not in a pond but a river. He did not die (although, in a sense, his character did when it was not renewed for the new season). And the only clue of a police connection came at the end of the dream, with the arrival of the police cars.

This peculiar mixture of real features and symbolic presentation is how all paranormal dreams operate. The mind seems to pick up a message and builds a little drama around it. I remember once that I dreamt about a flood and the need to escape from a tidal wave. I did so by drifting off on a passing piano. At the time I was discussing paranormal dreams with psychologist Dr Sue Blackmore of Bristol University. As the mind often uses puns, she wondered if I said in my dream, 'There's a flood – I need a ship to get out of here – who has ships? – how about P and O?' and this sequence, where the P & O shipping line was the first one that came to mind, was translated into a visual image of its pronunciation – a pi-an-o!

So perhaps Simon Slater unconsciously transmitted his experience to me. Or was my sleeping mind somehow able to tune into what the publicity department at Thames TV were planning to use as a promotion for their show?

This is not just idle speculation, because I had, in fact, written to about half a dozen TV publicity departments over the course of the preceding weeks. Quite a few had offered to put my letter on the noticeboard. In this way, any actors with experiences to tell could contact me direct. I had sent one to Thames TV, but out of all their possible programmes only *to the production team of* The Bill.

Doreen Sloane: '*Close*' Encounters of the Spooky Kind

Doreen was raised directly opposite Liverpool, on the Wirral peninsula, a wedge of land that juts out into the Irish Sea. This is an area I know well, living there myself for two years on the borders between Wallasey and Birkenhead, the only two towns of any substance in this quiet semi-rural area. It is clinging jealously to its Cheshire heritage, even though technically transferred to the new 'super-county' of Merseyside.

As the story that follows will illustrate, Doreen has not deserted her home and still lives within a mile or so of her birthplace, commuting daily 'across the water' (as locals put it) in order to reach West Derby. Here, amidst modern suburbia, you can find a housing estate built in 1981-2 by a well-known chain. It is like thousands of others all over Britain. Many real families live there. But they do so in peculiar harmony with constant TV stardom, for this Liverpool estate is unique in the world of TV soaps. One winding cul-de-sac called Brookside Close lies amongst all the rest. It has no occupants who pay mortgages, because they don't actually exist. Yet they are still known to millions of viewers in Britain, and several other countries. How is this? Mersey TV bought the entire section of the estate before completion. Most of it is used for administration offices and other purposes. All of it is guarded by security. However, a few dwellings at the far end of Brookside Close appear on air every week and are 'lived in' by a number of actors occupying the houses and bungalows in their fictional identities.

Doreen Sloane had no fewer than four separate roles in Coronation Street *and two in* Emmerdale Farm *before 1982. She was a natural for the character of Annabelle Collins. A well-to-do housewife and mother forced to go downmarket from her home on the Wirral when her screen husband lost his job. She became an original in* Brookside, *a sophisticated and unprecedented Channel 4 soap. Of course, in true soap tradition, she has since suffered many trials and tribulations, but the fabled events in her modest semi on this rather unusual estate are rivalled, if not surpassed by the realities that take place back across the Mersey in her real (and very different) home – a home occupied by something more than just her family.*

Doreen's real house is nothing like number 8 Brookside Close. It is a huge Victorian building in Oxton. Birkenhead, built in the 1890s for a large family believed to have been cottonbrokers. It has long since been divided into three flats, each one occupying an entire floor.

In 1978 Doreen and Len, her art-dealer husband, moved onto the top floor and set about converting it to their own needs. She recalls those early days: 'When we walked in, it just felt right. We said, "Yes, this is it. We have got to buy this." We simply felt that there was a lovely atmosphere and thought nothing more than that.'

But this complacency was soon to disappear. 'I suppose it started about six months after we moved in,' Doreen recalled. 'One simply felt there was something there. I have not had any experience like this before, so I can only say that it was very welcoming. But on this particular day I was in the kitchen when I *felt* someone walk behind me. It was not someone or something in the kitchen. It came *from* the hallway moving through to where the girls' bedroom is. And I thought – "Oh, somebody's come in." '

Doreen continued: 'I was standing with my back to the kitchen door, you see. To reach the girls' bedroom from the hall, you had to come past here.' It was someone doing this that she had felt, and why she naturally turned to see who it was. Her two sons did not live in the house, but her daughters, Sarah and Jane, were both staying there at the time, so she naturally assumed it to be one of them.

'I was alone in the house,' she noted, 'but I looked round just in time to see a dark shadow going into the girls' room. I thought it was one of them come home, even though I had not heard them. I called out "Sarah? Jane?" but there was no answer. So I went into the bedroom. They were not there. Nobody was. I considered this very odd, went back to the kitchen and thought nothing more about it. I mean, a shadow is just a shadow, isn't it?'

But this was not the end of matters; it proved to be just a beginning.

'I suppose it was three or four weeks later when the same thing happened again. This time the shadow actually went back.' Doreen explained: 'As I turned round, it went as far as the girls' door and then returned to the hall again – straight away. There was no sound at all.'

Afterwards Doreen saw the figure on a number of occasions. She offered a more detailed description: 'It was a definite shadow of an average-sized person. Completely black – *solid* black. Not so much an outline of a figure. You could not see all the features. It was not as definite. But it was about the size of a figure.'

We contemplated possible explanations for a moment. 'It can't have been a bus passing on the road outside, because we are too high – three storeys up.' Doreen grinned in her most pleasing fashion. 'It would have to be a very tall window-cleaner, I suppose, to throw a shadow like that.'

Doreen had quickly made up her mind that these various sightings were nothing natural. She was helped in this regard by the phantom smells that dominated the building. 'I would smell food cooking. At first I thought it was from the people in the flat below us, but they were away. And the people on the ground floor were actually out. But you could definitely smell it – something like stew and that sort of thing. A children's lunch, I would say.'

I enquired about the possibility of strong odours wafting on the breeze from a local take-out shop, but she dismissed the idea firmly and politely. 'No, we don't have anything like that. We do have a restaurant at a hotel a short distance away, but it was not that sort of smell. It was as if you were where they were cooking a children's dinner.'

Doreen digressed from here into what has become her own theory. Whilst the history of the house is uncertain, other than its long past occupancy by that large family, she has concluded: 'I think the house, when it was a house, had this floor for a nursery. The children actually ate up there and slept there, and their governess would feed them. I just have this fixation, really, that the house was owned by people who were very, very happy.'

She smiled at the thought. It obviously appealed to her, 'Yes,' she added, 'they like us being here. They are pleased we bought the flat. I know they are.'

Doreen laughed, but it was not a laugh that covered either uncertainty or unease. It was a genuine expression of warmth and affection for this now dead family from a distant generation.

These various incidents, none very strange in itself, added up over the months and years. Doreen comments: 'It was only about that time that I began to think that it all may be something – paranormal.' She paused to savour the term. 'That is a word I have only just learnt. I must say that before then I merely thought of ghosts.'

She seems perfectly happy using the expression 'ghost' and on several occasions left me in no doubt that this is what she sincerely believes to be the case. Her house *is* haunted. No question about it. But the ghosts are previous inhabitants and they do not mind the fact that she and her family have 'invaded' their territory.

Can this all be in her imagination? Being an actress, she must be quite gifted. Or have other family members had these spectral encounters as well?

'It is funny, because I had many of these experiences and I had not said anything to anybody. But then my eldest daughter was with me in the kitchen one day when I saw the shadow go past. I said quite naturally, "Oh! that must be the ghost," and she said, "So you've seen it too?" '

Sarah, aged twenty-six, is a presenter with Marcher Sound, the independent radio station just across the Dee estuary and wildlife haven of the sandflats that mark out the border with North Wales. She does not seem perturbed by the unexpected visitor to her bedroom and explained to her mother that it often came in. Jane, her sister, had seen it too, although not as frequently.

I was puzzled by this easy acceptance of an apparition in the room where they slept, but Doreen did not find it odd. 'They are not children any more, of course. And Sarah is very interested in the paranormal. Jane has since left home – not because of the ghost, I might add! She just decided to go to New York. Whilst Jane only saw it a couple of times, Sarah has seen it often.'

But what about Len, her husband? Doreen nodded. 'I mentioned it to him, and he said it was funny, because he had smelt cooking in our bedroom – which is at the other end of the flat. He told me, "There are often weird cooking smells throughout the house, and we know there is nobody else there and nobody has been cooking." '

In more recent times the spooky events have continued but moved into new directions. 'Whilst we never hear anything,' Doreen reminded me, 'the ghost does open doors and also stops us going through certain doors sometimes.'

Immediately I pointed out that sceptics would say that this might easily be explained by the wind. She shook her head. 'No. Obviously, the wind does open and shut doors, but there have been times when all the windows have been shut because it's winter. We have been in the sitting-room with the door closed – not on the latch, but closed to – and then it just pushes open. At first we thought the cat was doing it, but we've got up and checked and the cat wasn't there.'

By this stage in our conversation, I could see that those who debunk the paranormal would find little in this collection of anecdotes that would be particularly persuasive. They might regard the whole thing as wishful thinking and a *desire* to have a friendly ghost.

Whilst I was quite certain that Doreen was entirely sincere, and I could even see that she was aware of the way in which these incidents seem more trivial to those not involved, I had to ask her a crucial question. What was the one experience that most convinced her that something was going on that could not be explained by anything normal?

She thought for a moment, then began: 'We have walk-in cupboard in the sitting-room. I went in there for something one day. Sarah was in the room with me but over by the window. I did not close the door behind me, but when I turned round to come out again, the door *was* closed.'

Remembering the panic of the moment, Doreen's eyes burned bright.

'I turned the handle but I could not open the door. I called out, "Come on, Sarah – stop playing at pretending to be the ghost." Her voice came from far away and said, "I'm nowhere near the door." I insisted, "Very funny. Now stop fooling about." And Sarah, very insistent, replied, "I am looking out of the window. I am nowhere near the door." I tried again, but I could not open it. Then, all of a sudden, it just burst open.'

Doreen looked at me. I could see the frustration. 'I know the sceptics will say that it got stuck, but I did *not* close the door. I am *positive* it didn't stick. Absolutely positive.'

There have been other incidents with the same door. Once, Sarah was in the room – which is thirty feet long from end to end. She was doing her exercises and had her head underneath her legs. Suddenly she noticed that the wardrobe door was open. She was alone. It had definitely been shut before. So she stopped her exercises, stood up normally, and the wardrobe was closed again!

To my mind, the most intriguing experiences concerned Emma, Doreen's cat. 'Emma has funny turns,' Doreen said. But then she corrected herself: 'Well – no, she doesn't actually have turns. For a week, at six o'clock every evening, her hair stood on end and she could *see* something. She would run away – go to another room and try and get in – but then stop in the doorway and run back again, still with her hair on end. She was terrified. She ended up cowering under the dining-table which we keep in the hall.'

Animals are well known within psychic circles to be extremely sensitive like this. It is perfectly possible that Emma was picking up some sensation that was not detected by the family.

However, detected or not, it impressed Doreen, who was not keen to see Emma suffer. She told me: 'This went on for four nights. Now *this* will probably make the sceptics roar with laughter, but on the fifth night I had had enough. I was in on my own, and Emma was with me. So I just said to the empty space, "Please, ghost, you are frightening my cat. You can see how she reacts. She's terrified of you. Please don't do it." And Emma has not been frightened since.'

It is interesting that no one else in the other flats has ever noticed anything. Also Doreen's two boys, Angus and Bruce, have experienced nothing when they come to visit. 'They are very sceptical,' Doreen comments wryly. 'I feel that ghosts only ever appear to those who are receptive – those who are willing to believe.'

For this reason, Doreen considers it unlikely that we shall ever see an appearance by the spectre during one of her scenes in *Brookside*: 'It is very welcome to follow me on set, but I think it is attached to the house. We have never even seen him or her in the garden or the garage.'

Him or her? Doreen and Sarah have discussed this and concluded that it is most likely a woman in a long, dark skirt. But it is difficult to be certain, and they concede it might be a Victorian man in a frock coat.

The incidents continue to happen. Her husband heard the piano tinkle out a few notes when he was alone in the house. But the ghost was no great composer, and the tune was not up to much.

A few days before our interview, Len had had another experience. Doreen had gone to bed, leaving him alone in the sitting-room watching TV. 'The door was closed, but it opened three times on its own. It was not Emma. I had put her in the kitchen.'

We spent a few more minutes talking generally about the paranormal before the time came for a rehearsal with 'Paul', her screen husband. We went round to the 'real' Brookside Close, the few tiny houses you see during filming. Many questions still buzzed in the air. Doreen was genuinely fascinated.

'Do most people want to get rid of their ghosts?' she asked. 'Are they afraid of them? Am I just imagining it all? If so, how? Am I adopting the right attitude?'

I had to reassure her on this last point. She was remarkably well able to accommodate this apparition in her life, and, as she believes, this could well be why it seems to manifest so freely.

Doreen concluded: 'I don't want to get rid of it. I am just delighted that it is pleased we are here. I think it came back to check that everything is all right. But it is the ghost's house. The ghost was there first.'

Theme Music: Top of the Pops

After such a barrage of strange stories, you might find this chapter slightly out of place. What on earth have musicians to do with popular TV shows? Aside from the fact that music on TV provides many successful programmes (indeed, on satellite there is an entire channel given over to it), there are several reasons.

Musicians are stage performers. The difference between a popular singer or player and an actor is often difficult to spot (especially when on *Top of the Pops* they try to mime to their latest chart single!). This means that they can attract paranormal events, just as actors do. Their personality can open them up to receptivity.

Of course, some of you might prefer to think that this is all due to the drugs that notoriety would have them taking, but this is a misguided view. It is not true of the majority of musical artists, and the role of such artificial stimulants in the perception of strange phenomena is very much overstated in any case.

Additionally, quite a few musicians are developing their talents into acting. The story which I used in the introduction to this book is typical. Here was a rock musician who has appeared in TV soaps. You could apply the same definition to quite a few of his contemporaries.

David Bowie, for example, was fascinated by the paranormal in the sixties before he became an international recording star. He actually helped to put together a UFO journal, at a time when many weird lights in the sky were allegedly being observed over the Wiltshire town of Warminster. Quite how much this had to do with the regular military manoeuvres on Salisbury Plain is another matter entirely, but Warminster did become the world's leading tourist attraction for UFO-spotters during the 'flower power' days of 1967 and 1968.

Bowie went on to write music about the subject. His song 'Starman' tells of his belief that there are aliens watching the Earth and that they would like to come here but are 'scared they'll blow your mind'. Reflecting a truth that has become apparent over the years since then, he talks about the importance of children in this alien scheme of things – it has been obvious to UFO researchers that younger people are more likely to experience a close encounter. Indeed, leading New York expert Budd Hopkins, after studying hundreds of such cases, told me, 'Once you enter middle age, you are more or less safe. Being kidnapped by a UFO is a young person's game.'

David Bowie has since appeared as an actor in TV and movie projects, including the absorbing *The Man Who Fell To Earth*, where he plays an alien (with a British passport!).

Whilst I was working on this chapter, an interesting coincidence occurred. In late August 1988 I did a radio programme with the BBC in Nottingham (part of a series of shows throughout 1988 which I made with John Simons). One was on the subject of dreams. A man from Lenton Abbey phoned in to describe a dream he had had in the days when Bowie was developing his UFO interest. In it he saw a concert aboard a ship on the River Thames which the singer was then planning to give. Unknown to the performer, some people drowned in the water as the singing went on. That concert had taken place without incident, but in 1987, at another Bowie gig, the man's dream was horribly fulfilled and tragic deaths did happen. Some people apparently tried to swim over to an island off the coast of Ireland where the concert was being staged but ran into difficulties.

Others who have followed in David Bowie's acting footsteps include Sting and Genesis drummer and vocalist Phil Collins, who has even appeared in *Miami Vice*.

It is fascinating to note that many of these artists have written material about the paranormal and display considerable personal interest. Sting, for example, discuss the nature of the mind, ESP and synchronicity, and Genesis have produced tracks about UFOs (although *not*, as you might think, the one entitled 'Illegal Alien', which is about something entirely different).

Another in this line of actor/musicians is Toyah Wilcox. Her music is heavy with paranormal and science-fiction lyrics (for example, the hit single 'It's a Mystery'). However, she has blossomed to become even more successful as a TV actress, with appearances in series such as *Minder*. She was also in the last of a long line of Nigel Kneale *Quatermass* epics, which involved a theme of alien energies, stone circle sites, leys and mind-control.

A very interesting experience involving Toyah was described to me by a man I will call Phil, from Eccles in Lancashire.

It was the summer of 1985 and Toyah was in Manchester to give a concert. Phil met her in the city centre and requested her autograph. While she was confirming what words to put, 'She looked directly into my eyes,' Phil says and, 'Strange things began to happen.'

At the time the singer was well known for her garish make-up and extreme hair-styles and colouration. She was wearing a particular style then, but as their eyes met, Phil claims, it changed. The hair turned into a much more sedate fashion and reverted to black, which he took to be its natural hue. It was the sort of style she was soon to adopt as she expanded her serious acting roles.

Even the normally busy midday scenes on the bustling Portland Street began to fade away and the noise of people and traffic utterly vanished. This remarkably common feature of the paranormal is called the 'Oz Factor', as if Phil was temporarily pulled out of reality into a magical 'other world' (such as 'Oz'). Here, as he explains, everything was hazy '... except for Toyah's eyes. They seemed to grow and move towards me and almost filled my vision. A slight smile crept over her face as this began to happen.'

Phil speculates that Toyah *knew* that something was occurring all along. It is true that she is fascinated by the occult and in interviews has commented about her own ESP abilities, but was this a real two-way communication or just something the young autograph-hunter imagined? One thing is certain: he was not simply 'star-struck'. He tells me he has met many other celebrities, and this was the only time that anything like this happened, although he has had other telepathic encounters with members of his own family. This might suggest that the momentary rapport between Phil and Toyah could have extended into the psychic dimension.

As we might expect, the number of musicians who have had UFO experiences seems to be forever on the increase. Perhaps one of the most surprising is American entertainer Sammy Davis Junior. He actually became a friend of Dr J. Allen Hynek (who died in 1986), the man who single-handedly did probably the most to legitimize the UFO phenomenon. He was such a nice person to know that he befriended the famous and the not-so-famous with equal ease.

Davis seems to believe that UFOs are controlled by an intelligence which is friendly toward us. He has seen things on a number of occasions. Probably his closest encounter took place in Boston, when he was returning by car from a concert. He scrambled out onto the road to watch as the huge 'craft' with a dome on top hovered above him. It had different-coloured lights all around it, and it pulsated before climbing upwards and 'taking off'.

He is by no means the only one to encounter a UFO in such circumstances, probably because the nature of their work takes musicians out late at night on a regular basis. So, like police officers, often on patrol after dark, they are thrust into circumstances that are ripe for such strange experiences.

The rock group Hot Chocolate also observed a light in the sky on their return from a London concert. They were so impressed by what happened that they turned it into a song which became a number-one best-seller. To them there was 'No doubt about it', as their title said. Which is a sentiment often expressed by witnesses who do not have the ability to say it in such a lyrical manner.

Other records that feature UFOs as a theme have been made by many leading artists, from Crosby, Stills and Nash to the Carpenters. A classic double album by Dave Greenslade (known to many as the writer of theme music for hit TV series such as *A Very Peculiar Practice* and *Wipe*

Out) even attempts to describe contact with an alien civilization in a very evocative fashion. 'The Pentateuch of the Cosmogony' is the pretty dire title which masks a quite brilliant musical achievement, recreating something that is very hard to put across in any medium.

Probably the most interesting UFO encounter by a musician involved the ex-Beatle John Lennon, about which rumours have circulated for some years.

John Lennon was known to be captivated by the UFO subject, reading everything he could lay his hands on. He was an avid consumer of *Flying Saucer Review*, once widely considered the best UFO magazine in the world and produced from Britain for over thirty years. It started my own involvement within the field whilst I was still at school, and I was proud to serve long-term editor Charles Bowen in an administrative capacity for several years. In that time I learnt that John Lennon was by no means the only celebrity amongst the thousands who read it during the sixties and seventies.

The sleeve notes for Lennon's 1975 *Walls and Bridges* album say: 'I saw a UFO on August 23 1974 at 9.00 o'clock … J.L.' But very little else was known about the matter. These rumours came together in his final album, released soon after his murder in December 1980. The hit song 'Nobody told me' ('Strange days indeed') refers obliquely to there being '… UFOs over New York and I ain't too surprised'. Now we know the reason why!

The truth has been tracked down by researchers Harold Salkin and Tim Beckley. In 1988 they secured an interview with May Pang, who at the time was a very close friend of Lennon, acting as his assistant and living for over a year in his huge penthouse on New York's East 52nd Street.[23]

In fact, May Pang is a soap actress on the popular US daytime TV series *Another World*. She has also appeared in series shown in Britain, such as *The Equalizer*. It turns out that she was an eyewitness *with* John Lennon on that hot, sticky night in August 1974.

Lennon was out on his balcony overlooking the East River. He was stark naked – apparently not an unusual occurrence! He called May out onto the terrace, and they were both able to watch for eight minutes as the UFO approached, flew silently overhead and crossed the UN Plaza building (where four years later the United Nations held a debate on the UFO phenomenon). It then drifted off towards Brooklyn. The object was described as looking like a dark grey dome with a large red light on the top. The base was encircled by dozens of flashing white lights. It was absolutely silent, even at closest approach.

Of course, New York at 9 p.m. on an August night would be packed with people. How could something like this fly over without attracting the attention of the entire city? There were one or two other reports from in and around Manhattan Island, but when May called friends in Brooklyn as the object crossed the East River heading there, despite her telling them to go outside whilst she and Lennon were still watching the UFO, they were unable to see anything unusual.

Why was this? Does it imply that the UFO was 'real' only to those who saw it? Or are we to presume that it was something ordinary which most people recognized but Lennon and May Pang did not?

The description is exactly like a number of other UFO reports which have turned out upon investigation to be advertising-aircraft – slow-moving light planes that are strung up with brilliant lights in order to spell out messages. From certain angles the messages cannot be read, and they give the impression of a domed UFO. When seen correctly, the craft is obvious for what it is.

May Pang is adamant it was really a UFO. She says she took some photographs of it with her camera, which happened to be loaded with infra-red film. Unhappily, when developed, these did not show the UFO and appeared only to be strangely over-exposed.

Lennon, too, confided in his friend Elliot Mintz that this '... definitely wasn't an aircraft. It was a UFO.'

Despite his tragic murder in 1980, Lennon has lived on in many ways. As one of the most successful songwriters of the century, it was inevitable that he would do so. For example, he co-wrote the music ('All you need is love') which Britain used in the first ever global television programme, beamed in 1968 instantaneously around the world to many different nations thanks to new satellite technology.

But the strangest kind of immortality is the way in which Lennon has supposedly lived on, quite literally, in the realm to which mediums say we gravitate after physical death.

In *Beyond Explanation?* I did briefly introduce the trance messages of American psychic Bill Tenuto, who claims that John Lennon came to him in 1983 and used the vocal cords of the psychic to 'speak'. A passable version of the Merseyside songwriter, then three years dead, does come out onto the tapes of his 'experiments', which Tenuto sent to me.

It is interesting to assess the situation several years on, because Lennon (whether he was really communicating or whether it was an aspect of the medium's own personality) did make a number of specific comments about the late eighties. For a start, the eerie voice says: 'I am coming through in as many ways as I can ... giving my words to those who are wordy and my music to those who are musical.' Is there any evidence that this has occurred?

Consider the case of the musical medium Rosemary Brown. In the past she has produced compositions which she says were dictated to her by great masters such as Liszt and Beethoven. In 1987 she came forward with what she believes to be new melodies and lyrics that have been given her by John Lennon. This is precisely what was predicted via Bill Tenuto.

On the other hand, we still await the spiritual evolution that the voice of the former Liverpudlian promises in these sessions from beyond death: 'There's going to be a lot of turmoil. But there's going to be a lot of miracles too ... It's all coming out. ... There's a lot of purging to do.'

He speaks of growing awareness of, and interest in, the paranormal and contact with other intelligences. There has been some indication of that. In 1987 and 1988 three books about the paranormal featured in the top of the American best-seller lists. That is a state of affairs that has not occurred in the recent past.

Indeed, the major initiatives between East and West to bring about nuclear disarmament and the apparent moves towards liberalization in states such as the USSR could be further signs of Lennon's vindication.

I do not know whether the Bill Tenuto tapes are real evidence of Lennon's survival. I can only report that the medium has done everything he could to assist me. He told me that Yoko Ono was not very happy with his distribution of these messages reputedly from John – which I suppose is only to be expected. She cannot know their true nature.

Another thing which John Lennon (or Bill Tenuto) says in these tape-recorded sessions is that he (John) is working with a group of four or five dead people to try to bring peace and harmony to the Earth. One of them is American singer and movie star Elvis Presley.

Officially, Presley died of a heart attack on 16 August 1977, but there have been persistent claims that he is really alive (based on such minor things as a misspelling of his name on his gravestone). These have always been hotly denied by Presley's family although in late 1988 a brand new 'Elvis Presley' single making these claims was released in the USA! But according to John Lennon, 'the king' most certainly *is* on the other side.

Quite a few mediums agree with that sad diagnosis. As I write, in September 1988, a lady from Sheffield has just contacted me with the news that she has begun to receive song lyrics out of nowhere and fully formed in her mind. She was disturbed by this, because it had never happened to her before. Did it simply mean that she was unusually creative?

Apparently, a number of people more musically minded than she have commented that the lyrics (which she did not recognize) were in perfect beat. Someone I showed them to immediately suggested – without knowing details – that they appeared typical of an Elvis Presley song.

The case is still under investigation, but whether this is evidence of Elvis, like John Lennon, transmitting his music to a receptive mind is another matter. Perhaps his lyrics had just lodged in this woman's subconscious, without her realizing what they were. She categorically denies this and claims to have been no Presley fan.

However, it is not an isolated incident by any means. I have had letters from a woman called Pat who lives in

Vermont, USA, who wrote to inform me that events have made her convinced about the reality of the supernatural, but only since the death of Elvis Presley.

Pat has experienced many strange phenomena in connection with him – for example, memorabilia vanishing and reappearing. The most peculiar occurred in the summer of 1980, when a voice in Pat's head told her to return home. After 'hearing' it for several hours, she could resist no longer and did so. She was drawn to her bedroom, where a life-size poster of the singer still hung. Whilst she was standing beneath it, the voice quite distinctly told her: 'I am in you. You are in me. We are one. Because we are one, we can never be separated.'

So vivid was this 'thought' that she wrote it down immediately. But it meant nothing to her. However, sometime later she read a biography of Elvis Presley and discovered that he had been so fascinated by the philosophy of the mind that he had bought dozens of copies of his favourite esoteric book (which he had practically memorized) and given them away to all his friends.

The book, *The Impersonal Life*, was an obscure and deep tract about the spiritual nature of the self.[24] Pat finally tracked down a copy at a religious book store in Los Angeles. Inside the slim volume was the passage: 'You ... are in me and are one with me; just as I am in you. ... We are not separated. ... We could not possibly be separated.'

The words are so closely similar to those Pat had heard in her mind that summer's day in 1980 that she is convinced that they were transmitted to her by this member of what John Lennon calls 'the white brotherhood' – a union of famous personalities who are trying to impress their continued existence upon the Earth.

From that point of view, it is interesting to note that in what at first glance seems to be a Lennon and McCartney nonsense song about a walrus, from the Beatles era, we find the words. 'I am you, as you are me, as you are he and we are all together', which seems to express the same concept.

There are quite a few stories about the ghost of Elvis

Presley being seen by people on a tour of the family home, Graceland. Robert and Abigail Smith from Chicago report seeing him just a few inches away, though he was partially invisible. He was taking part in the 'tour' of his old home, wearing a white jumpsuit and sunglasses.

But even stranger than that is yet another comparison between John Lennon and Elvis Presley.

Presley has a daughter named Lisa. According to a recent story, 'She has become almost a carbon-copy of [Elvis], close friends report.'[25] Lisa lives under his spell and plays his records over and over. She has also consulted a leading psychic in Hollywood and believes that she has communed with the spirit of her father, who is helping to direct her life. In this, Lisa is uncannily similar to Julian Lennon, who appears not to have gone to such extremes but has written one song about a pact he was supposed to have engineered with John about communication after death. His musical style is also very akin to his father's.

Lisa Presley's mother, by the way, appears to be naturally concerned. She is, of course, very well known for her role as Jenna Wade in the TV soap opera *Dallas*.

Perhaps this is all a series of coincidences, but it is decidedly curious that (just as Lennon promises through the Bill Tenuto 'messages' both John Lennon and Elvis Presley are now apparently doing exactly what they said they would.

Episode Four: The Twilight Zone

Star Trek: To Boldly Go
Where No *Mind* Has Gone Before

If you have never seen Star Trek, *you must have spent the last twenty years in a Klingon detention cell. It began as a fairly mundane space opera, featuring the voyages of the* Starship Enterprise *several hundred years hence, as it bravely explores the universe and faces endless adventures. It simply caught the mood of the times as man reached the moon and dreamt of a day, beyond all our lifetimes, when the real exploration of other solar systems might begin. The show ran only a couple of series before being cancelled, but it became the most repeated TV series ever and turned into a cult. A new TV version, with a younger crew and a new starship, was a smash hit in 1987, but the original has also spawned a big-budget movie starring the original cast, and this has led to sequels,* Star Trek II, III, IV *and* V. *Rumour has it that, by the real date of the fictional* Starship Enterprise *mission, the actors will be making* Star Trek LXXX *from their bathchairs and cryogenic suspension tanks.*

It is really quite fascinating how many of the *Star Trek* team have had peculiar experiences. I related one previously, where DeForest Kelley supposedly used ESP to detect the 'astronomical' salary of Captain James T. Kirk (actor William Shatner),[26] but there are many others.

Leonard Nimoy, probably the best-known alien in the universe and (as Mr Spock) the one most in need of a good plastic surgeon, has presented documentaries on the paranormal and is certainly open-minded about these phenomena. Once, whilst living in Philadelphia, he visited a house that had been owned by the great writer of supernatural tales Edgar Allen Poe, and said that he detected a ghostly presence in his mind, as if the writer were somehow still there.

But it is in the field of UFOs that the starship's crew

seem most active. I suppose this could be because the *Enterprise* would make a pretty dandy UFO itself if it chanced to appear in our skies (and, come to think of it, they even wrote that into the plot of one *Star Trek* episode).

DeForest Kelley (Doctor McCoy in the show) had a close encounter in 1950, when he was driving through Louisiana. The cigar-shaped object whooshed through the sky, making a soft whistling noise, and seemed to sprout greenish flames from its rear. He says that, although it left a vapour trail behind it, this was no aircraft, because it possessed no wings.

However, it is William Shatner (ironically playing the archetypal American hero whilst being a Canadian himself) who reports the most amazing encounter. He has often expressed his belief that there could well be something in the UFO phenomenon and that real aliens, such as those he jousts with on TV, might actually exist. The reason for that is plain to see.

It happened some years ago, in the Mojave Desert of California, a hell-on-earth where temperatures can soar to such levels that you cannot survive for long unprotected.

It was 130°F as the sun beat down relentlessly. He had ridden out on a motorcycle along with four friends, and they were in the middle of nowhere, at the mercy of the elements. Stopping for respite and a very necessary drink of water, he let his friends ride on into the distance. Their machines glinted in the sun as they vanished over the roadless horizon.

With his thirst quenched, Shatner decided it was time to catch them up. His heart missed a beat when he realized that the motorcycle engine was not turning over. It was totally dead – as he would be himself if he did not find a way out of this mess very soon. He hoped that his friends would return, but they probably knew better than to get themselves lost by turning back. Besides, they had no immediate reason to think he was in danger.

After many frustrating minutes of trying to fix the machine, during which his canteen of water soon disappeared, he knew that he had to start moving. He pushed the heavy motorcycle, blindly trusting to luck that he was heading towards civilization rather than away from it, but the heat and exhaustion quickly got the better of him. Strong as he was, this was just too much, and he collapsed onto the ground, with concern turning rapidly into despair.

Then something flickered in the sky above. It was streamlined and made of shiny metal. It looked for all the world like a UFO.

As it moved away, he felt an urge in his mind that he should set off walking in a different direction. What was happening? It was as if some kind of telepathic voice was calling to him softly inside his head and encouraging him to keep going and to take a certain path. Perhaps, he thought foolishly, this was some alien intelligence connected with the UFO, and it was trying to rescue him.

He breathed in and gathered enough strength to let him move off with the motorbike. To his intense relief, a petrol station loomed up ahead and he was able to reach it, tired out but safe. After running-repairs, he returned home without ill effect.

William Shatner has often said about this quite remarkable rescue operation that he considers it very possible that his life was saved by the power of the mind and by alien beings.

These stories reflect the UFO phenomenon very well. DeForest Kelley tells of a wingless cigar which gave out a vapour trail. Whilst he thinks otherwise, most UFO researchers would probably expect this to be one of the nine out of ten sightings that do have an explanation. Maybe it was a jet aircraft on secret tests. It could even have been a fireball meteor, as these sometimes give out smoke trails. Wings can very easily seem to disappear when strong sunlight shines off bright metal.

But what of William Shatner's experience? That is an entirely different matter. It's what we call an either/or case. If it was accurately perceived (and heat exhaustion can effect one's senses, of course), it seems hard to explain as any obvious misperception.

The mind does possess wonderful resources, and it may not be necessary to imagine alien beings directing him along the right path when he could use ESP to do this for himself. But how much

nicer to believe that the Earth's favourite TV space voyager had
his life saved by a real voyager from outer space.

Shirley Stelfox: There It Goes Again

*Earlier in this book we met Don Henderson, alias the gritty TV
detective George Bulman. His face like a smiling rock masks an
actor who is really a loving and compassionate man frequently
tormented by his extraordinary psychic abilities. His wife and
companion since 1979 has been Shirley Stelfox, herself a
successful actress with many tales to relate. She very kindly
granted me a lengthy interview in which she shared for the first
time some of her experiences and her own feelings about this
strange way of life.*

Shirley was at the time (1987) a regular in the cast of
Brookside, *where she played Madge, the old-age pensioner who
was 'girlfriend' to both Harry and Ralph, two crusty so-and-so's
who are widowers and live together as a latter-day* Odd Couple
*(a series in which husband Don incidentally appeared). However,
she was just then filming her final scenes for the programme,
having been written out because, as she put it to me: 'I do not like
playing one character all the time, as you must in a soap.' In fact,
she was enthusing about a new movie she had recently completed
with award-winning actress Julie Walters. It appeared later in
1987 as the highly successful* Personal Services. *Shirley
implored me: 'Do go and see it. It is so funny.' And indeed it is. It
is based loosely on the Cynthia Paine story about goings-on in a
rather dodgy London establishment, and very few of her fans from*
Brookside *would have recognized their 'Madge'. Looking thirty
years younger and complete with sexy black underwear and
leather boots, one can only imagine what this sight would do to
·Harry and Ralph! Nevertheless, it was Shirley's soap image that
was the illusion. By which I do not mean to imply that Shirley is
a regular inhabitant of black undies. Nevertheless, she has some
way to go before collecting her old-age pension in real life.*

*After the interview, in 1988, she returned to TV screens in a
series about debt-collectors,* King and Castle, *which has shorter
runs than a soap opera, so gives her the freedom to express her
undoubted talents in a wide variety of acting parts on the stage*

and screen and in movies.

Shirley, like many actors, has had assorted brushes with the paranormal. She recalls a time when she visited a clairvoyant in London who had been recommended by others in her profession. Her name was Irene.

The psychic was a reader of Tarot cards – cards which have symbols on them that seem to act as a focus for innate abilities. This woman also supplemented her talents with psychometry, picking up impressions by holding an object that belongs to the sitter.

Shirley was puzzled by something the clairvoyant had told her: 'She described these two men in great detail. They were beautiful. Most unusual physically; in fact, in every way.' This baffled the actress, because she knew no one who remotely fitted this description, let alone two such people.

'I told the clairvoyant I did not know the men, and she just smiled and said, "You will." Well, six months later I was doing theatre work in Worthing and was having drinks in the "Toby Jug" with the rest of the cast after the performance. Suddenly, there were these two men. They were exquisitely beautiful. They were so stunning that we talked to them and discovered they are brothers. They have become extremely close friends of mine, but it was only afterwards I remembered the words of the clairvoyant. She had described them down to the last detail.'

However, it is since her marriage to Don Henderson that strange things have really taken over.

The most vivid of Don Henderson's visions was one which Shirley Stelfox shared directly. Neither of them fully understands what happened, but Shirley admits: 'It could be that Don saved my life with this one.'

The family live in a house on a busy road in Warwickshire. Traffic in that part of the world is often heavy, particularly in the summer and at weekends. As Shirley tells it: 'One Saturday morning our daughter Louise, who was a Brownie, had to go somewhere. It was not far, so Don agreed to drive her, but he was very worried about parking when he came back. If you leave the space outside our house free for any length of time, somebody snatches it. Then you have to search for ages to find an alternative spot.'

This was a common occurrence, as Shirley noted. They had devised a solution: 'Our neighbour had driven his daughter too, so his wife and I got two chairs, placed them at the edge of the road to protect the parking-spots and sat there chatting to one another waiting for our husbands to return.'

'Shortly, her friend's husband returned and stopped. Don was coming up just behind but, instead of pulling in, he seemed to slow, then accelerate and shot straight past.'

The three of them looked at one another, puzzled, but concluded that he must have forgotten something and was driving back to collect it. So Shirley and her neighbour continued their vigil in the chairs and got on with their conversation.

After many minutes the phone rang inside the house. Leaving the chair standing guard, Shirley rushed indoors to answer. She was more than a little astonished when she discovered it was Don, phoning from a call-box.

He was angry: 'What on earth are you doing? You were supposed to be protecting the space with a chair.'

'I was. I still am!' Shirley protested.

'No, you aren't. There's a big white car in my space. I had to drive past.'

Utterly perplexed, Shirley said: 'What are you talking about? The space is free. I've been out there all the time. There's no white car.'

'Yes, there is!' Don insisted. He went on insisting it *had* been there.

Eventually she persuaded him to return home. He had been driving round in circles looking for another place to park, he explained. But he now accepted that no white car was parked outside their house. Nevertheless, he insisted that, when he drove by and then accelerated on, this had been because he *had* seen such a vehicle parked there. It was as clear as day.

The issue was resolved only with the assistance of the two neighbours, who confirmed that when Don had arrived back and driven past they had been out there with

Shirley and the parking-space had definitely been free.

Shrugging off this little mystery and putting it down merely to an idiosyncrasy, Shirley went into town to do some afternoon shopping. She piled her trolley high with bags of food. As any busy shopper will know, negotiating the streets with one of those when your hands are full is no easy exercise. The road was very busy, so it was necessary to keep a careful eye on the traffic.

At the same spot an elderly couple were also attempting to cross. The man was taking the highway code seriously, looking both ways and observing the stream of cars with great concern. The woman seemed to adopt the philosophy of setting off and hoping that any traffic not detected would see her first and draw to a halt.

Unfortunately, it did not work out that way. A car appeared on her blind side and struck the elderly woman a glancing blow shortly after she stepped off the kerb. In front of Shirley's horrified eyes, the woman was cast into the air and crashed down onto the pavement.

Luckily the car was not travelling very fast in the snarled traffic, and the woman was suffering more from shock than serious injury. Whilst someone went to call an ambulance, Shirley hastened back into the greengrocer's and asked the manager for a chair so the accident victim could sit down.

As the chair was brought out and Shirley helped the woman to settle into it and await medical attention, the truly weird nature of the events now struck home.

This chair was remarkably like the one she had used earlier to guard the parking-spot. It was now placed on the edge of the road, just as her chair had been three hours before. What was even more peculiar, the car that had done the deed was very distinctive. It was a large white one!

'I really do not know what to make out of all this,' Shirley acknowledges. 'It was truly extraordinary the way these things all blended together. How Don had seen the car and the chair mixed up in that experience just hours before. I wondered if the person struck by the car might not have been meant to be me. Perhaps I paid more attention to the road subconsciously. Or, if I had understood the meaning of his vision immediately after it had happened, would I have been able to prevent the woman's walking right into the car?'

It is tempting to think through a situation in this way. However, the reality is much less easier to figure out.

It would seem likely that the coincidence of the similarities between the chairs was just that: a coincidence. But it acted as the trigger in Don Henderson's mind.

Whilst you are driving, the mind tends to enter an altered state of consciousness quite naturally. It becomes a routine operation, and when you are alone, it is very easy to drift into a sort of 'automatic pilot' stage. This could well be a state where the drawbridge rises up more easily and ripples from the future can sneak through.

Don's being aware of the accident that his wife would very nearly undergo and that she was soon about to witness at first hand, the experience of seeing the chair in the road linked in with this coming incident (which was also to involve a chair). The whole affair flooded into Don Henderson's subconscious mind but, instead of his previewing it exactly as it would be, the one image that got across the barrier was that of the big white car. So this became superimposed upon the scene in Don's eyes at that moment and he thought he saw the car actually outside his house in his parking-spot.

Very likely there was nothing either of them could have done to use this precognition in a positive manner. That is one of the most worrying aspects of this kind of paranormal experience: what possible purpose does it serve if the act of foreseeing the future achieves nothing of any value? No one seems to have an answer to that question. All that Shirley Stelfox knows is that the events happened as just recounted.

As she told me in summation: 'You can scoff about this as much as you please, but the fact is, it happened, and there is no way that something like that can be explained away as chance or circumstance.'

Fred Talbot: Under the Weather

When I first met Fred, he was a science teacher in Altrincham, Cheshire. He was lucky enough to be asked to host The Final Frontier, *an ITV series of children's programmes on outer space. In 1982 we enjoyed putting together a feature on UFOs for one of them. Soon after, Fred quit teaching to go on tour as a professional lecturer, but this was aborted when he was offered the job of weatherman by Granada TV. His smiling optimism, plus the clear evidence from his forecasts that he knew 'just as much' about the weather as most British TV meteorologists, won the hearts of viewers and he quickly grew into a media personality. His assignments have become more and more taxing, and he now appears on other networked ITV shows, from quizzes to magazine formats. He has also had the dirty job (someone has to do it) of making exchange weather-forecasting visits to TV channels in Denver and Australia.*

Fred is liked because he epitomizes the fairy tale that anyone can become a TV star, with nothing more than natural charm and by being in the right place at the right time. As a TV 'Cinderella', his jovial arm-waving personality has made him into a figure of fun, who provides entertainment for the masses (especially when he is driving around in his amazing sardine-can bubble-car – which the Americans would not allow him to drive on their roads!). What more can you ask for on TV these days?

It was the day in June 1988 best remembered for being the one on which the British summer fell that year. Fred Talbot and intrepid TV reporter Steve Winstanley were in the early stages of a televisual experience – cruising by barge along the canals and waterways of north-west England.

This was always a brave or foolish mission to undertake. Unlike a ride down the Amazon by canoe, where the heat can be guaranteed, or an icy plunge through Himalayan cataracts, the waterways cruise might be roasting or freezing. The climate of England in June is unpredictable even for a weatherman. Despite the weather Talbot and

Winstanley sailed on merrily, negotiating the discarded bedsteads with deft (or daft?) precision to send back film of their encounters with local characters.

Yet on this particular day they were to meet a character not in the script. They nearly had a scoop by interviewing a poltergeist.

The scene was set in a series of three tunnels that stretch over a mile between Daresbury and Preston Brook on the outskirts of Warrington. It is a very forbidding run, as the low roof and narrowness engulf you along with the pitch dark. It is easy to imagine all kinds of ghouls in there. The tunnels are also reputed to be haunted in local legend, although that may be because any sound reverberates back upon itself, with hollow echoes through the silence and isolation.

According to first reports reaching me, as they were chugging along, two empty baked-bean tins rose from the rubbish bag on deck and literally jumped over the side of the boat. They fell into the water with an ominous plop. The two men were in the middle of their journey. There was nothing they could do but continue the long, slow crawl towards the light. Being trapped in the inky black with this weird force was more than enough for anyone.

Fred, an admitted sceptic on the paranormal and a 'rational, science-minded person', was convinced there would be a natural explanation, such as a touch of the wind coming down the tunnel's air vents – although he did admit the tins *appeared* to climb vertically upwards. The younger reporter, Steve Winstanley, was reputedly having kittens by this stage and categorically insisted he would never venture into that tunnel again.

Predictably the Granada TV press office saw the potential and advised that baked beans are well known for generating wind, hence the most likely explanation. But, as I suspected, this turned out to be more in keeping with their wish to manufacture appropriate headlines than hard fact, so I decided to see what Steve Winstanley had to say about this ghostly encounter.

First he confirmed that it was no gimmick. It really *did* take place. 'It has been exaggerated a bit by the press office,' he told me. 'For a start, it was not baked beans tins but two cans of beer. Maybe they did not want to create the impression we were seeing things whilst we were tanked up on expenses.'

Steve was, of course, adamant that this was in no way the case. 'It was probably nothing. I guess it was likely the wind through the tunnel, causing a vacuum or suction effect. But it was a bit frightening at the time, and especially when you knew – as we did before going in there – that people have gone in and never come out again. They've *died* in that tunnel.'

I could see that another part of the exaggeration was Steve's refusal to go back in the tunnel – period. He was clearly not overjoyed about the prospect but was reacting calmly after having had a several-week period to think about things.

But then he added a surprise: 'You know, something else happened that we never reported. Earlier, in the same tunnel system, we were followed by what sounded like a very strange animal. We could not see anything, but we heard the noises. They were really weird, not at all like the little scufflings that might have suggested a rat. This was bigger, much bigger.'

I pointed out that I had lived in the Warrington area myself and that once a badger had come near our house. Might it not have been one of those?

He hesitated, then answered rather too slowly: 'Yes – that will be it.' But he was not fooling anyone, least of all himself.

This story is typical of how a tale can grow in the telling and take on new proportions. Yet, despite the attempted hype, there clearly was something at the heart of it. Perhaps as the two men were doing their best to rationalize, it was all a series of unrelated and quite explicable events. A water creature might have been swimming beside the boat, attracted by their left-over food, and with its noises echoing in the peculiar acoustics of that accursed place. Maybe the animal even got inside the rubbish bag and accidentally nosed the beer cans skywards as it proceeded on its rummage. Or, as Fred proposed, the wind whipped through the tunnel in a swirling vortex that flicked up the garbage with its tongue.

Given the spooky atmosphere generated by the darkness and the known history of the place, who could be blamed for wondering if there might not be a more supernatural origin for the events?

And yet ... There is just a little more to this than meets the eye. Something that neither Fred Talbot nor Steve Winstanley seemed to know. This was not the only weird episode to occur in that small part of Cheshire.

In researching a series of cases were people suffered strange lapses of time, I came across one that had happened there. The witness, a contractor from Stockport, had been driving through the tiny village of Daresbury when his car engine conked out. It happened again the next night. And on the third occasion he suddenly 'came to' with nearly two hours having vanished and forty miles away from his intended route – on the edge of Preston, the administrative centre of Lancashire. There was much more to this story, including ghosts and strange dreams.[27]

No sooner had I got all this on record than another story came to my attention. A young woman driving home from Liverpool turned off the M56 motorway at Preston Brook, just above the haunted tunnels. She meant to head through Daresbury and so home, but on the sliproad she lost all sense of time and 'came to' further down the exit route and seven hours later. Her car and legs were covered in mud, but she did not know how it had got there.

This bizarre case took on new dimensions when someone (certainly not I) leaked it to the national press and reported that the woman was kidnapped by a UFO.[28] Many of the later press stories were wild exaggerations – quoting me when I spoke to none of the papers! Quite a lot of material shows how the truth here was far more complex than the tabloids imagined.

However, one thing seems inescapable. There is no obvious way that the woman who lost those hours could have known about the Stockport man's time travel and teleportation (which was not publicized). Nor is it likely that the two Granada TV presenters knew of either previous event.

The woman in the second case thought that a nuclear establishment that sits in nearby fields might be responsible. Were they up to some sort of dastardly experiment, she speculated. Whilst I doubt it, something else occurred to me, which I mentioned to none of these four witnesses. Daresbury is a tiny place, perhaps famous for only one thing: it was the *birthplace of a man whose pen-name was Lewis Carroll and who wrote immortal stories about a young girl named Alice, who fell into a tunnel and entered a magical 'looking-glass' world he termed 'Wonderland', where time and space disappeared. And, it seems, they still do.*

Terry Treloar: An Actor's Life

In the course of researching this book, I came across many stories involving actors. In some cases this led to long correspondence, when I realized that the actor was just as much interested in the whys and wherefores of his or her experience as I was. Terry Treloar was an example. He wrote to me after finding one of my books through a peculiar incident at the mobile library in his Essex village, where the book 'popped out' of the shelf at him. I realized from all the wonderful curls in his writing and vivid story-telling ability that here was a man who was the archetype of the psychic and the actor, and living proof of the link between the two. Whilst you may not recognize his name instantly, he has appeared on TV often, for example in Hi De Hi, Jenny's War *and* Inside Story.

'As an actor, in the last few years I have developed an unfortunate sense that I did not realize I had until I read your book,' Terry told me. He can instantly sum up whether he is doing well or badly during an audition. He seems able to 'tune in' to the emotions of the producers and know whether there is a rapport.

This is crucial, I think. When coupled with a number of other clues he has offered about his experiences, it shows how actors open themselves up to 'read' emotions. They 'drink in' images and impressions, turn them into visual pictures and so undergo a paranormal experience.

For instance, Terry believes that his moods are easily influenced by whether he picks up positive or negative thought. He has an extremely vivid night life and often dreams lucidly – that is, he *knows* he is dreaming during the dream itself.

He described one experience, when experimenting with

his ability to create vivid images: 'I laid down on my bed for a moment … suddenly I seemed to be in a dark tunnel. I seemed to have been there for some time and I could smell damp earth and see in the dim light thick roots coming from the walls. … Then I saw an exit, a large oval, and I seemed to see sunshine … the exit was above me, the way out of the dark into the sun. At this point the whole thing suddenly turned itself off.'

Of course, Terry realizes this might just have been imagination, but he insists it seemed very real. Most interesting to me was his note that the sound of an ice-cream van outside the house just faded away. Indeed, all sounds of the normal world had done so, to return as the experience ended. This isolation – like being briefly sucked out into 'wonderland' (or Oz) – is the Oz Factor again and is a classic symptom of a psychic experience. Note too how the tunnel and the light at its end feature in the near-death encounter of Stephanie Beacham – and, indeed, in many other out-of-body experiences or UFO abductions. That is surely significant.

Terry also adds, very innocently, that animals seem attracted to him and wonders if this is in any way connected with their apparent ability to sense through ESP much more readily than humans.[29]

One nice incident that illustrates this is described by Terry. He begins: 'It could be imagination or faulty vision, I suppose – although I have excellent perception and an eye for detail that is very necessary in my job. Sometimes I see things that are not there, and vice versa.'

In late 1986 he was sat alone in his living-room watching a video on TV when he noticed something on the floor. He turned, and there was his large ginger tomcat, sitting on the carpet. 'I saw him quite clearly, and he vanished just as if a switch were thrown.' The cat had died just a year before.

As to the reverse process, he mentioned a time in May 1986 when he was directing summer entertainments in Ayr, Scotland. One of the girls in the cast had recently become engaged and was proud of her ring and fond of showing it off. But one day in rehearsals he saw it was not there. He started to exclaim that it must have slipped off when he realized it *was* there, as plain as day.

Terry considers this ability *not* to see something that everyone else *can* see as psychic. His impression is that the mind, having sensed the fact that this engagement would be a brief one, dramatized that intuitive knowledge by overriding his senses and making the ring vanish. A very similar process works in an altered state of consciousness (the hypnotic trance) when people can be 'persuaded' *not* to see a chair, for instance.

After the summer season was over, a better explanation came to light quite unexpectedly. Terry suddenly had a feeling in his mind that the girl was in trouble. On impulse he wrote to her, and she replied. Terry kindly let me examine this letter, in which she says: 'I don't know how you knew something was wrong. You must be telepathic or something.' Her London flat had been burgled and all her jewellery stolen – hence, quite possibly, the reason why Terry saw the ring 'vanish' a few months before.

This demonstrates how the mind's use of symbols to describe information that it obtains by psychic means can create problems of translation. The interpretation that the vanishing ring meant that the girl's engagement would end was a logical one, but it turned out that something else, which fitted better, had possibly been foreseen. The message had been about the theft and had got through but it was simply read incorrectly.

Terry is an old friend of Don Henderson, who, as we have seen, is another very psychic actor. They met many years ago, when both were co-opted to help out with a performance of a Tennessee Williams play at a drama education centre in Walthamstow, East London.

Terry was doing a spot of teaching there and, with a couple of volunteers, decided to ignore the failure of the authorities to provide funding to spruce up the canteen, and paint it themselves.

It was a dark November evening, and they worked on into the night. Suddenly, footsteps began to echo up the old stone steps. The one colleague with him at that point heard nothing, but they checked anyway. The building was deserted. About an hour later the sounds came again. This time the other man did hear them.

A third person arrived later to help finish the job, but it

was 2 a.m. before they did so. Exhausted, they were standing in the middle of the canteen floor, preparing to go home, when one man called for silence. They all edged to the middle of the room and clearly heard male and female voices, mumbling, as if reciting something in unison. They came from a darkened 'classroom' at the far end of the room.

Slowly they made their way towards it. Opening the door, they plunged the room into light. The voices ceased. No one was there. The building was deserted. Later, when they reported it to the caretaker, he admitted that things like this had happened before. He had heard noises and voices too when the old building was empty at night. Doors and windows had even unlocked themselves mysteriously.

Years later, Terry had more or less forgotten about these events. He now lived out on the Essex coast and was appearing in a pantomime in Kent. One day, when he was being driven back to London by the director's assistant, to while away the time he told her about the strange goings-on at Walthamstow. She did not know of the place and was unfamiliar with the area but was so engrossed by the tale that she lost concentration on the road. The woman soon realized she had got herself lost.

But Terry Treloar was not lost. They were driving straight up the road towards the little back street where the haunted drama school lay in wait.

Dick Van Dyke: Cloud Busting, Daddy

I recall Dick Van Dyke from his TV comedy shows more years ago than I really care to recount. And he is still going strong, white hair and all, with his own brand of American humour. But he may well be best known for his marvellous film portrayals. Who can forget the magic scenes with Julie Andrews in Mary Poppins, *when, as the only Victorian London chimneysweep whose accent came from Manhattan instead of Maida Vale, he danced and sang with cartoon characters and flew through the air? Well, as you will see, the real Van Dyke claims some rather unusual abilities too.*

In about 1973, during a wave of UFO experiences in the USA, the Van Dyke household was invaded.[30]

Mrs Marjorie Van Dyke saw them first. Indeed, she was so determined to prove their existence that she woke husband and children up and eventually purchased a telescope so she could watch them more closely.

They were described as looking like cylinders that manoeuvred around the sky in an erratic fashion. Dick described them as having flashing blue and green lights which, it was speculated, came from the windows in the sides of the objects which blinked as they rotated past.

In fact, Dick Van Dyke was convinced that his wife was psychic. He explained that Marjorie was forever able to predict who was about to phone and was also rather good at finding objects that had become lost, simply by the power of her mind.

But it is the Mary Poppins abilities of Dick himself that are the most amazing. He is reported as claiming that it is possible to burn holes in clouds just by concentrating hard enough. He says he has trained himself to look at even the worst storm clouds and disperse them merely by staring at them. He focuses his attention, and normally within a minute or so a hole begins to appear, showing blue sky in a perfectly round patch.

No doubt you find this claim somewhat extraordinary, but Dick van Dyke is by no means the only one to allege that it is possible. Some years ago a man named William Reich even proposed that he had discovered a new type of energy, which he called Orgone, and that by concentration it was possible to focus this on clouds and make them disperse. His 'cloud-busting' technique (as he called it) received a lot of attention, and there are all sorts of stories about official pressure to hush him up.

Singer-songwriter Kate Bush whose fascination with and deep knowledge of the paranormal are obvious if you listen to her music, even wrote a song entitled 'Cloud Busting' on her masterwork 1985 album Hounds of Love *(which, incidentally, has an entire twenty-five-minute side devoted to a long expression of her ideas about ESP, the subconscious mind, ghosts, reincarnation and the spirit). Most people were utterly bemused by the lyrics of such songs, but Dick Van Dyke would probably understand them well enough.*

Bill Waddington: Not Like Percy Sugden

The essence of every soap opera has to be its characters. Without them there is no way that viewers around the world would tune in every week for years on end. In each programme you often find that the same types of personality tend to be portrayed, and actor Bill Waddington plays a very popular one – the grumpy old man who is a perpetual busybody.

Born in Oldham in the Pennine Hills, this great old stager first appeared on TV in 1946 and has been a regular for some years in the cast of Coronation Street *– termed 'the best-loved soap in the world' (and the longest running). In Britain alone it still attracts an enormous 20 million audience. This Granada show is still (few would deny) the most popular TV series of its ilk. Where it scores is in its ability to present the real life of a Salford terraced street and blend good-quality storylines with far more humour than other soaps can muster. But it is not the humour of the situation comedy. 'The Street's' sense of fun emerges from its characters. Bill Waddington's 'Percy Sugden' is a perfect example: crotchety, always getting in the way, forever interfering and insisting that he knows it all. Yet beneath all that lies a warm-hearted soul who is loved as well as loathed and for whom most people really do have a soft spot – even if once or twice we might be tempted to suggest it ought to be the marshes at the back of Canal Street.*

A great deal of 'The Street's' rich love of life pours from Bill Waddington. He told me at the start of our conversation (which I wouldn't dream of demeaning by calling an interview): 'I am not like Percy Sugden. Not like him at all.' You can judge for yourself in the pages that follow, but after Bill had bombarded me with ideas, suggestions, speculations and anecdotes I felt as overwhelmed as any resident of Weatherfield who has faced a dose of Percy's chatter. Far more than with any other actor I talked to in my work, Bill left me with the distinct impression that he was just like the character he reflects – all the nice parts of Percy Sugden, anyhow.

'These stories that I've heard about you – are they true?'

I asked my first question of Bill rather warily, more than half expecting to be told they were stuff and nonsense. My contact at the Granada publicity office had seemed to imply that he thought many of them were.

'Oh yes,' the actor's thick northern accent proclaimed. 'Everything you have heard about me will be right.'

As it turned out, that was certainly an understatement. There had been a few rumblings in the local press about Bill's agreeing to open a psychics' fayre that had recently been held. It all seemed a lot of fuss over nothing to me, particularly as the event raised money for charity and as the critics mostly contributed nothing – bar their prejudice.

However, Bill Waddington had perfectly honourable reasons for his support, irrespective of the fund-raising purpose: his own experiences had left him fascinated by the whole subject.

'Let me tell you this,' he explained. 'These things have happened to me, but I don't understand them. I find myself saying things to people – friends and the like – about certain events. Then, after I have said them, they look at me surprised. All I can say is, "How did I know that? Why did I say it?" But I just do. I just seem to know things about people and come right out and tell them instinctively.'

I asked for an illustration and was assured that they happen all the time. The most recent he could recall took place a few days before our chat (which, by pure coincidence – although the irony was not lost on us, took place on Hallowe'en 1988).

A close lady friend (Bill has many, and I can see why!) had come to him because she had lost something precious. It was an antique gold ear-ring. She was distraught but bold as anything he announced: 'No, dear, you haven't lost it, only misplaced it.' Then he proceeded to explain that it was still in the room where she had last seen it, but it had become covered up. She had already searched everywhere, and this seemed most unlikely, but Bill was adamant. A day or so later it turned up, just as predicted, hidden under some egg cosies which must have accidentally been placed on top.

'I knew it was there,' Bill said, beaming. This kind of conviction is by no means unusual with him.

He mused about the implications of this ability: 'I love the company of women, you know. They seem to have an extra sense which men don't possess. Yet I can sense things about people. I tend to take them as I first see them. But I can come across a person who has done nothing to hurt me and yet I just don't like them. It's a kind of spiritual sense. Just a way of feeling their inner self.'

I remarked that I had noticed this sort of thing with many people and that it was especially prevalent amongst actors, hence my research for this book. It blends into empathy, and this in turn can often lead to a sort of telepathic rapport, especially with a loved one. That seems to be why psychic experiences are most common between mother and child, husband and wife, and so on. No emotional bond is greater than love, and emotion is the catalyst of all forms of ESP.

Bill understood that: 'I meet some people and they try to cover up their true emotions. There is something wrong with them, for instance, but they are just not showing it. Yet I always *know* if they are upset. They cannot hide it from me. I also get intuitions about people and things, I instinctively know when something will turn out all right.'

As with most people who have this innate psychic talent, Bill experiences a very vivid dream life. We smiled through a few of his more memorable nocturnal adventures, some of which would be a little too outrageous for dramatization on *Coronation Street*!

So far as he could recall, he has had no premonitions, but he did say: 'I often sense that something has happened before.' He was describing the feeling of *déjà vu*, a French term meaning 'already seen', and a remarkably common occurrence. 'Whilst I cannot say before something happens what it is going to be, I can sometimes know if a nice thing is on the way.'

Bill displayed another characteristic I have come across

very frequently in people with enhanced ESP abilities – a rapport with other forms of life.

'I love animals,' he said. 'I have bred racehorses for over twenty years, and I go to see them every weekend.' He paused a moment, then added, matter-of-factly, 'I talk to them all the time, you know. I'm not afraid of what people think.'

He described an occasion when he phoned his trainer to ask about Lucy, a prize horse. 'She's all right,' came the news. So Bill said, 'Yes – but what about last night?' The trainer admitted that Lucy had been off her food. Although he had been miles apart from her, Bill had sensed this: 'I knew it. I always know instinctively if something isn't right with them.'

In the soap, Bill's character, Percy Sugden, is forever boring neighbours with his tales of 'what I did during the war'. Fictionally he was in the catering corps. In reality, Bill was an entertainer who toured the battlefields. His unusual abilities helped out even then.

'Once I remember being sent to a tank unit that had lost most of its men. Those who were left were in a very bad way. The stress was enormous. I was shell-shocked myself just being there and seeing the aftermath. But somehow I seemed to absorb their feelings. It was as if I took the burden upon myself.'

I suggested that it was rather like being a sponge and soaking up all the negative emotions, and he warmed to the analogy: 'Yes, I can't even remember what I said or what I did. I just stood there and took it into myself.'

In a way, although he may not realize this, and Bill never suggested it, he was behaving just as a medium might operate. By going into an altered state of consciousness (a 'trance'), it is possible to shut out recognition of the conscious world and react on a more emotional level to 'heal' the terrible scars that were affecting those troops.

Such was the turmoil of those days that Bill was packed off to see 'the chief psychiatrist of Scotland Yard'. Very quickly he reassured me: 'I wasn't barmy, you know,' and grinned, 'In those days a lot of people needed help.' But his ESP seems to have made Bill especially vulnerable.

The psychiatrist passed him fit for further duty but posed an interesting question that Bill Waddington still believes was important: 'Have you any twins in the family?'

'I had two twin sisters who died during the last years of the First World War in an epidemic. They died within a week of one another. I doubt I would have been born but for that. In a way, I came along to help my parents get over the tragedy.'

The psychiatrist explained that it was noted in clinical experience that having a history of twins in the family was a common factor in people who displayed ESP. It is easy to see why. Twins are bonded together in a very special way, and many studies have shown how often one shares the other's pains and knows what the other is doing even when they are physically apart.

'They can feel one another's emotions,' Bill pointed out. 'Twins seem to be in tune, just as I can get in tune with other people.'

I wondered if he had ever been tempted to use this ability in some professional form, but Bill did not seem to think he was in any way special.

'I remember a few years ago, just before I heard I had the part in *Coronation Street*. I was in a pantomime at Liverpool, and the principal girl in the production stared at me from the wings. She just said, "Your best things in acting are yet to come." ' Bill grinned at the memory: 'At my age, that was a little unexpected.'

The role of Percy Sugden was confirmed shortly afterwards, and when he saw the actress again, he was reminded of her amazing success. 'But she couldn't recall a thing. She just did not know that she had said anything.'

As a diversion, Bill has picked up the habit of reading tea-leaves. 'My father used to do it. And as a spot of fun I started reading for friends. I soon got a reputation, because a few things I told them came true.'

Once, when he was contemplating the purchase of farmland on the Pennines between Lancashire and Yorkshire, he stayed in a hostelry. 'I read the leaves for the landlord and said, "You're not going to be here very long. You are going to a hotel with a church built on top of it." '

This seemingly peculiar statement was vindicated several weeks later, when an unexpected move took the landlord to a new establishment in Oldham which was located in such a way that the sloping land behind the building created the illusion that a church was growing out of the roof.

'I've done it again a few times since then. I told one family that I saw the image of a pram and a baby in the cup. So I decided there was going to be a new child born. That day their daughter was taken into hospital. She was past normal child-bearing age, and the prognosis of the doctors was that it was a growth. Of course, it wasn't. It turned out that she was pregnant.'

This ability seems to be nothing more than a focus for his own intuition, reading the symbols as others might interpret dreams or ink-blots. But it has an attendant risk, which he acknowledges: 'I treat all this as just a bit of fun, but that creates problems when you get it right. Because I can do it and I don't know how I can do it, people tend to think that I am God. Of course, I am no such thing.'

One of the purposes of this book has been to explore the question of whether there is a link between acting and ESP. In my view that conclusion is inevitable, and I had to ask what Bill Waddington felt.

'Actors must have good intuition,' he noted. 'If you're in the profession, you are always living at least two lives.'

I told him of some other people I had interviewed. There are similarities, for instance, with the comments of Jean Rogers, and I strongly recommended that he take any future chance to talk to Michael Bentine. 'I would love the opportunity. I've met him once, and I know he is interested.'

I assured Bill that it was more than interest, and that Michael was exceptionally knowledgeable and understanding of the field.

'Actors and actresses have to take on another person's mantle,' Bill speculated. 'I have to let Percy Sugden come through me. It doesn't happen naturally. In a way I am letting the spirit of a different person operate through my body.'

Again, of course, this is precisely what mediums profess

to do, and I suspect that there are major clues in that correlation.

We talked a little about the role of Percy, and he was delighted that after some effort the writers had been persuaded to add a new dimension to the character. 'At last they have given me something to do that others can be sympathetic for. So I have to find a way to make that happen. I have to take on the right mood and let it show in my face.'

He added as an aside that actors also tended to be very superstitious, clinging to memorabilia and mementoes. This brought the subject around to his late wife and the little model she had made of the character he was playing when they first met, just after the war. He still takes it everywhere.

His wife had passed away in 1980, but the link between them was as strong as ever. 'If I need to feel depressed for my part, I think about my wife, and it all comes flooding through. I believe she helps me. She says to me, "Don't worry. Everything will be all right." '

I was fascinated by this. Was Bill suggesting that his wife's spirit was in some sense still connected with him and helping out in his *Coronation Street* acting? It did seem so. 'My daughter has done an oil painting of her, and if I am ever in a quandary – if there is something that I have to resolve, I go and speak to her picture.'

As if recognizing the way this must sound, Bill assured me: 'I speak to myself a lot. I'm not at all ashamed. I always feel when I talk to that painting that she is there helping me out in some way. I sometimes think that she is trying to convince me of an afterlife.'

This was the most extraordinary admission, although Bill had always been remarkably frank and open, with commendable honesty. He confirmed that his wife had been interested in the concepts of survival after death and of contact through mediums.

'I used to ridicule Spiritualism. Now I believe there is something to it. After the sort of experiences I have had, you have to. But I am not dabbling in the occult, as some people have accused me. That's just ridiculous.'

Perhaps those who criticized Bill's support for mediums

might have reacted differently had they bothered to try to understand the man and see why he felt as he did. It was clear to me that his attitude was based on more than wishful thinking.

I explained how it was always frustrating for me as a serious writer to find my books labelled 'occult' in a store. I *never* write occult books, only books about strange human experiences and our attempts to understand them. In my view, the audience is very different. There is a tendency to regard 'the occult' as black magic, and spells, and that is an automatic turn-off for most responsible people. Why we, as a society, cannot learn to treat the paranormal on the same level as we treat other fascinating human questions worries Bill Waddington as much as it does me.

Bill remarked: 'One vicar has criticized me in public because of my association with occult groups. But why? Can anyone come forward and say they have seen God? Could this vicar do so? So what is he talking about? How can the things which happen to me be occult? Have these Christians never heard of the Holy Spirit?'

Our conversation had drifted on, and it was now approaching the familiar time of 7.30 p.m. on a Monday, when for so many years households across Britain have tuned in to the strains of the *Coronation Street* theme music.

I politely reminded Bill of this. He chirped: 'I never watch unless I'm in it. But I think I am in it a bit this week.'

He left me with many things to ponder, including the thought that, if more people were as open about their experiences as Bill Waddington, most of the stigma still attached to this subject would very quickly be swept away.

'It's just that my mind happens to be open,' he explained with a trace of regret. 'Some people are frightened by these things. How can they understand it if they shut the door and refuse to listen? I am not afraid. I just wish I knew more about it.'

Lindsay Wagner: Bionic or Psychic?

The star of numerous movies, Lindsay became a regular on many people's TV screens around the world when she played The Bionic Woman, *reconstructed out of microchips by a team of surgeons and given amazing powers. Yet the irony is that Lindsay possesses even more amazing powers than her TV character could dream of – all without more bionics than the fantastic super-computer which is the human brain.*

Just about the most disturbing story I came across in my research involved Lindsay Wagner back in 1979. But there is an interesting prequel to that famous tale.

It started with a dream. A twenty-three-year-old manager at a car-rental firm kept having it night after night. It was the same one. He heard a noise like engines failing, then saw a plane topple over and crash into a horrific fireball. The searing heat of the flames shook him awake. David Booth, the man who had these terrible nightmares, was petrified. What did they mean? He was not intending to travel by aircraft. No accident took place. Yet these images were so vivid and real.

Eventually Booth was forced by his own conscience to phone the Federal Aviation Administration. The FAA were kind, but what could they do? Here was a man raving on about a dream. They could hardly take any notice of that. But he did have a clue. The silver-grey paint and the insignia on the tailplane suggested that an American Airlines plane was the victim, so he phoned them as well. Finally, perhaps pondering the meaning of it all, he phoned a psychiatrist interested in dreams at the nearby University of Cincinnati.

All these calls were remembered by their recipients afterwards. They occurred on 22 May 1979. But no one could *do* anything, and the poor man felt no better. The dreams went on happening. Tuesday night's nightmare, followed by the Wednesday and Thursday as well. Then they stopped. He said: 'There was never any doubt to me that something was going to happen. It wasn't like a dream. It was like I was standing there watching the whole thing.'

On Friday 25 May 1979, without knowing about these private dreams of David Booth – which had not been publicized in any way, Lindsay Wagner was at Chicago's O'Hare Airport. She was booked with her mother onto an American Airlines flight. But after checking in, and with just ten minutes left before stepping on board the giant DC-10 jet, she was swept with a feeling of doom. Lindsay knew that there would be a tragedy and begged her mother to let her switch their reservations.

Lindsay's mother was disturbed. This was not the first psychic flash her daughter had undergone. At the age of fourteen she had seen a brief image of a house, which she was able to describe in great detail. It turned out to be the one she and her husband later bought, although it was several years before she saw it in actuality.

So mother and daughter took this vision of disaster with great seriousness and decided not to board the DC-10. The plane took off, lost an engine as it climbed steeply, inverted itself and crashed in a ball of fire just off the end of the runway. Everyone on board – all 273 people – died instantly in the worst aviation accident on American soil.

But several people survived. They later came forward to say they had missed the plane because of forebodings. And the two most celebrated and grateful survivors had failed to board only because of a premonition: Lindsay Wagner and her mother.

As for David Booth, he heard about the crash and was horrified and distraught. He felt shattered at having been quite unable to prevent the catastrophe. Jack Barker, a public relations officer with the FAA, confirmed that the call had been made three days before the disaster and that many of the details Booth had described fitted the subsequent plane crash exactly. He saw the airline, even described the DC-10, knew it would lose an engine and topple over and even saw the crash site very accurately.

It was uncanny. But, as the FAA pointed out, what could they have done about it? There was no way they could have grounded every American Airlines aircraft for an indefinite period. In this instance, seeing the future in almost every detail had not been sufficient to prevent the tragedy.

Lindsay Wagner never doubted her psychic potential after this experience. Indeed, when her young son Alex was born in late 1987, she immediately had him checked out to see if he had inherited her talents. Early in 1988 she visited a psychic researcher who channels messages about people through a 'spirit guide', a Red Indian warrior. The warrior confirmed her suspicions. When Alex grows up, he will become a great medium, she was advised. His words will bring many blessings to the world.

An interesting question is posed by this premonition. If the plane had *been grounded and had never crashed, there would not have been an accurate premonition in the first place. Does this mean that our future is fixed and unchangeable? Or is it simply large-scale events that cannot be prevented, whilst individual destinies, such as that of Lindsay Wagner, can be steered around the fate?*

Billie Whitelaw: Tuning In

A wonderful and many-faceted actress, Billie Whitelaw (voted best British actress in 1989) has appeared in countless stage and TV productions. She starred in the mini-series Imaginary Friends, *taking the role of the leader of a sect which received messages of power. Just a few weeks before that TV series went on the air, Billie was working with me on a project designed to test ESP – a subject she has reason to be fascinated by.*

Billie's role as a sort of 'white witch' in *Imaginary Friends* was very apt, because that is what her husband, Robert, actually calls her, thanks to her ability to sense the future before it happens, with beneficial results. Indeed, she believes that she owes the life of her husband and four-year-old son to the powers of her mind.

In her son's case, she suddenly had an impression in her head that something was not quite right. It grew from a sort of gut-reaction to a desire to watch him intently. This turned out to be exactly the right thing to do, because he had contracted meningitis, without showing any obvious symptoms. Nevertheless, her acute senses insisted that she get the doctor immediately. She did so, and he arrived in time to steer Matthew through the worst and to put him on the road to recovery.

Her husband also owes his health, quite possibly his life, to Billie's ESP. They were on holiday in France one July, well away from other people, when he complained of indigestion after a huge meal. Most of us would have regarded this as a reasonable probability, which would pass in time, but Billie 'knew' it was more serious and had always sensed that Robert might suffer a heart attack. The doctor was called, and he had indeed suffered such an attack. Only her prompt action meant that the doctor was on hand to prevent a second, almost certainly fatal, coronary.

This was the background with which Billie approached the ESP experiment that I set up. I was, in fact, working with the women's magazine *She*, in a controlled test which we tied in with the publication of my book about ESP, *Sixth Sense*.

The idea was this. A series of photographs of famous people were displayed in the magazine. Readers were then advised that one – and only one – of these celebrities would be taking part in an ESP experiment on a given date at a given time. They were asked to 'tune in' and try to achieve two things: first, to identify which of the personalities was taking part, and secondly to sense the details of the environment from which the celebrity would be attempting to tune in to the readers.

We were very careful to balance the pictures of men and women. All were TV personalities in one way or another. Only the staff at *She*, I and, of course, Billie Whitelaw knew which of the six faces really was attempting to exercise ESP. The other five, incidentally, were newscaster Jan Leeming, impressionist Faith Brown, chat-show host Terry Wogan, presenter Frank Bough and *Yes, Prime Minister* comedy actor Paul Eddington. Even in the unlikely event that readers had known about Billie

Whitelaw's ESP experiences (which were not publicized beforehand), they would still have had to balance this against Faith Brown's experiences, which were far more widely known at the time.[31]

According to the notes made by Billie Whitelaw during the experiment (noon, 15 February 1987), she was picturing the view from her country cottage in the Stour Valley, with its whitewashed walls, and an arched wicker gate into a garden with roses, apple and cherry trees and daffodils in full bloom. More details were added of the kitchen, with its wooden table and beige curtains with blue and green roses. Certainly there was more than enough specific detail to test ESP. Would Billie's ESP be able to project these thoughts, and would other people be able to use their psychic powers to pick up the information? I was hoping that, by involving many folk all at once, through *She* magazine, we would be able to offer some meaningful overall results.

But just what happened?

The method I suggested was to 'dowse', by dangling a chain or locket over the photographs and note when it started to revolve. This appears to work because the ESP occurs as a sort of 'mental twitch' inside, which is then magnified in a physical way – by the fingers allowing the locket to twirl when the subconscious announces that it should do.

Since there were six possibilities, chance decreed that, for the hundred or so detailed entrants, around sixteen or seventeen should have guessed each particular celebrity. In fact, it might have been argued that some particularly prominent personalities (for example, Terry Wogan, then on TV almost all the time!) might have been chosen more often. But the results proved otherwise, Terry Wogan was actually the lowest of the six by quite some margin.

We could split the results according to the sexes, since there were three male and three female celebrities. Of course, being a women's magazine, most of the entrants were women, so this probably biased the results but, even so, fifty-four per cent chose a woman, as opposed to forty-six per cent selecting a man.

As for Billie Whitelaw herself, she really did come out

top of the poll. In fact, an amazing twenty-three per cent of those who entered decided that *she* was the person who was taking part in the experiment! That result is well above chance level and offers very strong evidence for some psychic factor being at work.

However, there was another mini-experiment built in. Twenty of the respondents decided not to take part by 'tuning in' on the day but instead to try an alternative test – for precognition. They had to decide *before* the date of the experiment, either by picking up images from their dreams or via some other intuitive response, who would do the sending when the day came. Then they sent in this 'prediction', having their letters postmarked before the date when the session took place.

Incredibly, this was even more successful. Fully seventy per cent went for a woman in this sample, and all of forty per cent (well over half those who chose a woman) were spot on in deciding it would be Billie Whitelaw!

But what about the actual impressions of images that were being transmitted. This was, of course, rather more difficult to judge accurately, yet a great many people did seem to do very well.

Probably the most successful were a husband-and-wife team of mediums from Kent, who came up with so many correct details it was uncanny. They got the gardens, the whitewashed walls, the wicker arch and the daffodils exactly right.

There was no suggestion that this was a serious scientific experiment. It was largely a spot of fun and an attempt to involve a lot of people in testing their own ESP. Billie Whitelaw is to be thanked for being brave enough to help demonstrate that there are indeed hidden depths to the human mind which too many scientists are ignoring.

But the 'ESP-eriment' (as *She* described it) was also designed to show that the testing of psychic potential could (and, in my view, should) be removed from the laboratories. It is all very well asking people to guess what card comes next or which random number a computer is about to generate in some long series of deathly dull sessions. This may produce statistical results that convince scientists, but it is not how ESP works in real life.

As our many reported experiences from actors in this book serve well to demonstrate, ESP occurs suddenly, out of the blue and in real situations which are often very dramatic. I believe that the best way to prove to those who are sceptical that this can happen *to you* is to conduct large-scale experiments such as this, which are fun and exciting, and in the process duplicate as best we can how ESP functions in the real world.

One lady who took part in this test really said it all when she explained why she had chosen what turned out to be the wrong person. She added, 'A tiny voice in my mind said it would be Billie Whitelaw, but I ignored it.'

Using ESP in real life is all about *not* ignoring that tiny voice, which we might call intuition, a gut feeling, a vague impression – or psychic powers. This tiny voice is what can sometimes make the difference between life and death. Ask Lindsay Wagner, Billie Whitelaw and many other people.

Bruce Willis: Moonflighting?

One of the surprise TV hits from America in recent years has been Moonlighting, *a decidedly off-beat story of a rundown detective agency operated by a rich former model and with a dishy chief investigator strolling through episodes like a zombie in a trance, cracking one-liners with the speed of an automatic machine-gun. Cybill Shephard (whom we briefly came across earlier) plays the model, and Bruce Willis, who rose from obscurity to multi-millionaire status, the wacky detective.*

According to experienced reporter David Bromfield, Bruce Willis is very different from the character he plays in *Moonlighting*. Instead of being an outgoing, ever-playful centre of attention, he is in reality of a very down-to-earth and introverted man, who is a proud father of a baby born in the summer of 1988 and who lives for her and wife Demi Moore.

Bruce Willis is clearly not at home amid the glitzy lights of Los Angeles. He would prefer to live in the country and not to have to face the hectic schedule imposed by the shooting of a TV series. Indeed, he has vowed to leave the hugely popular soap – whatever money is offered him – during 1989.

Against this we have to contrast the curious stories that have emerged about his alleged obsession with alien abductions.

According to sources close to Bruce, he became very interested in the whole subject during 1988 – so much so that Demi has allegedly become rather worried about the consequences. She apparently does not mind the fact that he is fascinated by stories of people who claim to have been taken for a ride inside a UFO, but Bruce has reportedly told some people that he would not mind being an abductee himself and that the prospect of this occurring seems a very real one. Indeed, he has reportedly stood watching the sky for hours from his apartment.

In his work on *Moonlighting*, Bruce Willis has made an enormous amount of money, some of which he has invested back into film projects with which he is either directly or indirectly associated. Throughout 1988 a number of movies on the UFO and alien kidnap theme were being developed in the USA, and Bruce expressed some interest in them because of his fascination with the realities of the subject.

According to one British newspaper, these stories, which appear to have some substance, go even deeper. They claimed, in a headline tale 'Heart-throb's Alien Kidnap Scare!', that '... the macho star ... believes star-struck Martians want to whisk him off to another planet to appear in a space soap.' Apparently Demi has even gone to the extent of banning him from watching *Lost in Space* re-runs on TV because of his obsession with the idea that he will be picked up and carted off. The story added that Bruce was very upset at having missed the lead role in one of the true-life abduction movies, due to pressure of work on *Moonlighting*. He had presumably hoped that this might get the idea out of his system. However, his belief in UFOs and aliens seems to be very sincere, and he has apparently argued passionately in favour of these perplexing 'technological angels'.

Just how much of this is moonflighting and how much reality is difficult to ascertain. Certainly, I anticipate that at least some of it is media exaggeration.

One delightful tabloid, the **Sunday Sport,** *has become a national institution with its amusing and extraordinary paranormal yarns. For instance, we were told of a woman who ate a UFO by mistake when she took it for an aspirin. Then there was the case of the mother ready to give birth to an eight-pound trout after a rather fishy abduction by aliens. Or how about the poor boy turned into an olive by a UFO ray gun, only to be eaten by the investigating police officer as he was sipping a martini?*

Do you find yourself questioning whether these claims might perhaps take an occasional liberty? Some people are bound to wonder about the veracity of the World War II bomber plane successfully photographed on the moon (around the same time the Sport *was giving a world exclusive on the first authentic pictures of Heaven). Yet there is no doubt that some of the* Sport's *claims have checked out. I followed up one or two seemingly wild reports as a test and found that, whilst exaggerated, they usually had some semblance of reality behind them.*

However if anyone feels victimized, I doubt they mind too much and will likely put it down to experience.

I have even been subjected to the treatment myself. In early 1988 the Sunday Sport *told readers that my soon-to-be-published book contained lots of stories about 'bonking aliens' who were invading Britain on a 'lust hunt' to discover nubile young women. I am not at all sure from where they got their (mildly inaccurate) information – it certainly wasn't from me or the publishers. Doubtless the story led to a few rather disappointed readers when they read my much more sober presentation of the facts.*

Still, I have to agree that it did no harm to the sales figures!

As we go press the Sport *has just announced an intergalactic scoop: ' "I had sex with aliens," says top Hollywood star.' Bruce Willis's co-star Cybill Shepherd has allegedly recalled under hypnosis being 'raped' by UFOnauts. They apparently told her, 'We only need you for a genetic experiment.'*

Stay tuned to this channel, or outer space.

Fading Titles

So there you have it. A mixed bag of strange tales for you to take or leave. I doubt if those persuaded will be in any way surprised. I do not expect the sceptic to be converted either. One of the first laws of the supernatural would appear to be 'Those who experience, believe, but those who simply speculate prefer a seat on the fence.'

I cannot argue with that. It is everyone's right to make their own decisions about the nature of the universe.

However, whilst some of the tales in this book are thin, perhaps even suspect, and may be open to other interpretations, I saw enough in my travels to satisfy me that certain phenomena beyond current science actually *do* exist.

I was particularly impressed with Michael Bentine's grasp of reality. Go back and read that interview. I think it is rich in ideas that you can dwell upon as a source of contemplation.

Other royal roads to truth – (such as tarot cards or astrology) are in my opinion nothing but lenses which focus our own inner talents. The cards themselves produce nothing; it is our inherent capacity for ESP, our secret double life at the level of consciousness, which provides all the answers and only uses these symbols to spell out messages.

The mind does not function in mathematics and logic. It ticks according to different laws which use another (often dormant) part of the brain as its filter into reality. These laws involve feeling and imagery. Inevitably those who live their lives immersed in these sensations experience what the rest of us wave away as the paranormal.

It is *not abnormal*. Nor is it *rare*. It is commonplace and fundamentally a part of each one of us. The trouble is that some folk prefer to wish it away with a magic wand, to hide the facts beneath a smokescreen of prejudice and fearful indignation.

The superstitious are *not* those who accept what experience of the real world dictates but those who pretend not to.

Every one of us has the capacity to experience. Most often this comes by way of dreams.

In my dreams I have witnessed out-of-body states, clear premonitions of the future, and the power of visual imagery that can override all other senses. And I am by no means what people tend to deride as a psychic – for want of inventing a name to camouflage our basic lack of comprehension.

This happens so often and to so many of us that the most astonishing thing is not that there *is* truth behind the para-normal but that we do not embrace this exciting fact with more enthusiasm. Instead we force those who do take note to comply with arbitrary rules and 'prove' it in a laboratory.

These rules are an excuse, an occult spell as powerful as any mumbo-jumbo we might be accused of uttering. They are created by hypocritical scientists willing to return home, fall in love, go to church on Sunday and praise a God that defies every law of nature, then pop into the laboratory and work with atoms no one can ever see or point a telescope into the universe and murmur incantations about infinity, fifth and sixth dimensions and time flowing backwards.

Place those same scientists in a room with someone who dares recount a psychic experience and what happens? They will gag, choke and rummage desperately for a get-out clause. This is not possible, they will implore. There are no scientific rules that allow it. You cannot have invisible forces or telepathic contact!

But you *can* have love, God and nuclear physics.

Just the day I write these closing lines it has been announced that the comedy actor Roy Kinnear (recent star of a TV show entitled *The Clairvoyant*, in which he played a dubious medium) has died after a tragic accident. This was during the shooting of the new movie *The Last Return of the Four Musketeers* (see p.123). Kinnear was only fifty-four, and his death was a great shock.

Just a year before this September 1988 incident, Ken Phillips, a London researcher, contacted me. He was desperate to put on record an awful premonition. It had come to him from a woman, who had dreamt of Roy Kinnear's filming a scene and dying in a terrible accident. The scene did *not* involve a fall from a horse (as the actor's death did in actuality), but all the other components were there. Here you do not have to take my word. The witness was so upset by her dream that she took the precaution of telling several researchers about it. Moreover, Ken Phillips wrote to the actor himself, offering what he suspected would be a futile warning to take care. All this was documented with me in the summer of 1987.

Actors dying during the filming of scenes is a thankfully uncommon happening. Roy Kinnear would by no means be an obvious name that would occur to you when a film star springs to mind. And at his relatively early age, death by natural causes would not be considered probable.

The debunker will point to the one-year gap and the difference between the dream (which involved a water accident) and the subsequent dry-land reality. Although the actor's death did have incidental connections with water, it should be noted. These facts, they will insist, illustrate that – impressive as it sounds – this was all just one more coincidence.

As this book shows, actors may seem to display this talent more often than others, but this is merely because their professionalism requires a raising of the drawbridge in their minds, to let in the emotional, intuitive (in other words 'psychic') information that flows through us all the time.

This force is neither mysterious nor sacrilegious. It is part of the wonderful, beautiful thing that has been shaped by destiny into a human being. That we are only now making the first gentle footsteps into our second self – the world of consciousness – is but an inevitable product of our steady, deterministic route towards scientific progress.

The universe is full of wonders that await our discovery. Everything comes when its time is right. This *is* the time to conquer our fear of the paranormal and stride on towards appreciation and understanding.

Closing Credits

I would like to acknowledge all those who assisted in the preparation of this book. The researchers who gave me their ideas. The actors who shared their encounters. The TV production and publicity offices who assisted in my quest for information.

I hate singling anyone out, but it is only fair to mention the assistance of the following: researchers Tim Beckley in the USA, Bill Chalker in Australia and Jon Padgen in the UK; Jane Wastie at the Theatre Royal in Bath; Joyce Hopkirk and Jane Hardy at *She* magazine; Briony Barton at BBC North-West; Graham King at Granada TV; Janice Troup at Brookside Productions Mersey TV; Kathy Campbell at JNP Films, Australia, and the press teams at Yorkshire TV and MTM, Studio City, California.

Also thanks to June Brown, Stuart Hall, Susie Mathis and Billie Whitelaw for being prepared to stick their necks out and take part in my open-ended experiments – which could have had any outcome.

Finally, a thank-you to those actors who were kind enough to send me their good wishes for this project, even though they had no paranormal experiences to report themselves:

Michael Elphick (*Boon*), whose regret was sincere, even though his hotel is reputedly haunted.

Terence Alexander (*Bergerac*) and Nerys Hughes (*District Nurse*), who offered their warm regards for the collection.

Nigel Hawthorne (*Yes, Prime Minister*), who said that he found it a 'very interesting' project.

Tom Watts (*EastEnders*), who was kind enough to explain that he has sadly '… never had any experience of bumps in the night'.

And Guy Siner (*'Allo! 'Allo!*) who was at pains to point out: 'Alas, while I have had many strange experiences, I am afraid none of them have relevance to your field of research.' If you've seen the show, you'll know exactly what he means.

Anyone wishing to develop their interest in strange phenomena can contact the following organizations (with an SAE) for more information:

BRITAIN: ASSAP (Association for the Scientific Study of Anomalous Phenomena), 65 Amersham Road, High Wycombe, Bucks HP13 5AA
BUFORA (British UFO Research Association), 16 South Way, Burgess Hill, Sussex RH15 9ST

USA: Archaeus Project, 2402 University Avenue, St Paul, Minnesota 55114
CUFOS (Dr J Allen Hynek Center for UFO Studies), 2457 W. Peterson Avenue, Chicago, Illinois 60659

AUSTRALIA: ACUFOS (Australian Centre for UFO Studies – and paranormal events) PO Box 728, Lane Cove, New South Wales 2066

Readers can also report any experiences direct to me (in confidence if required). Please enclose an SAE if you would like an answer: 37 Heathbank Road, Cheadle Heath, Stockport, Cheshire SK3 0UP

Sources cited in the text

1 Quoted in L. Funke and J. Booth, *Actors Talking About Acting* (Random House, USA, 1961)
2 Quoted in H. Burton (ed.), *Acting in the Sixties* (BBC Books, 1970)
3 J. Randles, *Sixth Sense* (Robert Hale, 1987)
4 M. Sabom, *Return from Death* (Corgi, 1982)
5 M. Bentine, *The Door Marked Summer* and *The Doors of the Mind* (Grafton, 1981 and 1984)
6 R. Moody, *Life After Life* (Bantam, 1975)
7 B. Hopkins, *Intruders* (Random House, USA, 1987; Sphere, UK, 1988)

8 J. Randles and P. Hough, *Death by Supernatural Causes?* (Grafton, 1988)

9 J. Randles and P. Warrington, 'The Neglected Science of UFOs', in *New Scientist*, 10 February 1983

10 *Don't Fall Off the Mountain* (1979), *You Can't Get There From Here* (1981), *Out on a Limb* (1983), *Dancing in the Light* (1986) and *It's All in the Playing* (1988; all Bantam)

11 P. Devereux, *Earthlights* (Thorsons, 1982); also his updated chapter in H. Evans and J. Spencer (eds.), *Phenomenon* (Futura, 1988)

12 J. Randles, *Abduction* (Robert Hale, UK, 1988; Inner Light, USA, 1989; Headline, UK, 1989)

13 J. Randles, *The UFO Conspiracy* (Cassell, UK, 1987; Sterling, USA, 1987; Javelin, UK, 1988; Capricorn, Australia, 1988)

14 D. Stokes and L. Dearsley, *Joyful Voices* (Futura, 1987)

15 For press accounts, see, for example, M. Streeter and T. Hynds, 'James Dean Death Wish of EastEnder' in *People*, 1 May 1988

16 S. Absalon, 'Anita Dobson To Quit' in *Daily Mail*, 10 February 1988

17 R. Davis (ed.), *I've Seen a Ghost* (Grafton, 1975)

18 C. Wilson, *Poltergeist* (Grafton, 1986)

19 See the report on the psychometry experiment with which I was involved, conducted by Dr John Dale at Manchester University, in J. Randles, *Sixth Sense*, op. cit.

20 J. Randles, *Beyond Explanation?* (Robert Hale, UK, 1985; Random House, USA, 1986; Ravette, UK, 1986; Bantam, USA, 1987)

21 A. Green, *Our Haunted Kingdom* (Wolfe, 1973; Fontana, 1974)

22 Interviewed by S. Feinstein for the *Sunday People*

23 R. Brown, *Look Beyond Tomorrow* (London, 1987)

24 *The Impersonal Life* (Sun Publishing, USA, 1941 and 1967)

25 *Celebrity* (magazine), 11 August 1988

26 J. Randles, *Beyond Explanation?*, op. cit.

27 J. Randles, *Abduction*, op. cit.

28 For the media version, see M. Keenan in *Chat* (magazine), 18 June 1988, and the very different version in *Northern UFO News*, April/May 1988 (available c/o the author)

29 D. Bardens, *Psychic Animals* (Robert Hale, 1987)

30 *True UFO Magazine*, winter 1977

31 J. Randles, *Beyond Explanation?*, op. cit.

General Index

Index of Celebrities and Series